Praise for
As My Age Then Was, So I Understood Them

"Stephen Corey's *As My Age Then Was, So I Understood Them* is some-times bookish, in the best ways, and in addition to welcoming many of the stars in our pantheon (Shakespeare, O'Keeffe, Keats, Ginsberg, Woolf, and Whitman for example) there's also the dual elegy for the poet's father and Dickinson (the latter also has her own baseball poem), Emerson 'at the moment of his first masturbation,' and a sequence in which Li Po and Tu Fu hop on a jet and tour America. What this means is that when Corey forays into 'the real world' —keeping a hospital death watch, exploring and exalting carnal love, or delighting in his young daughter 'playing Beethoven on my chest' — the poems are in-formed by both of his masters… by the 'shelves of books ' that are 'the bones of my brain.' "

—Albert Goldbarth

"'Here is a life, and a life, and / a life,' Stephen Corey writes in the opening poem's instructions to on how find the faded leaf—also a metaphor for the end of life—that one must imagine still colored after he is 'gone.' The poem is echoed near the end of this stunningly rich and encompassing book in a poem addressed to his four daughters about what he has missed during his life. In between we encounter a world we thought we knew but have not seen in this way before: things as varied as Monarch butterflies, telephones, calligraphy, and bread, as well as other writers and texts that become lenses to show us 'How we are growing undoes what we are' and see.

Like the glassblower's art in one of these major poems, 'Breath makes another world.' And like his Michelangelo in a sequence that masterfully covers centuries, we see 'the way a life we love can be steered, / beyond our control, beyond us.' And so, thanks to this im-portant and needed book we too can live beyond ourselves; that, indeed, is the highest praise for any art."

—Richard Jackson,
author of *Broken Horizons* and *Where the Wind Comes From*

As My Age Then Was,
So I Understood Them

New and Selected Poems

1981–2021

Stephen Corey

WHITE PINE PRESS / BUFFALO, NEW YORK

White Pine Press
P.O. Box 236
Buffalo, NY 14201
www.whitepine.org

Publication of this book was supported by a grant from the National Endowment for the Arts, which believes that a great nation deserves great art; by public funds from the New York State Council on the Arts, with the support of Governor Kathy Hochul and the New York State Legislature, a State Agency; and with funds from The Amazon Literary Partnership.

Printed and bound in the United States of America.

Cover Photograph: The abandoned Ontario Power Company's generating station, Niagara Gorge, Niagara Falls, Ontario, Canada. Built in 1905, the station ceased operations in 1999 and is now owned by The Niagara Parks Commission. Photograph copyright © 2021 by Elaine LaMattina.

ISBN 978-1-945680-53-3

Library of Congress Control Number: 2020952141

The title of this book is from
"Apology for Smectymnuus" by John Milton (1642).

Acknowledgments

My thanks, first, to the presses and editors who published my earlier books:

The Last Magician (1981), winner of the Watermark Press First Book Award—Charles Fishman and Coco Gordon, editors.

Synchronized Swimming (1984), winner of the Swallow's Tale Press Book Award—Joe Taylor, editor, who reissued through Swallow's Tale both *The Last Magician* (1987) and *Synchronized Swimming* (1993).

All These Lands You Call One Country (1992), University of Missouri Press—Beverly Jarrett, director.

There Is No Finished World (2003), White Pine Press—Dennis Maloney and Elaine LaMattina, editors.

*

And thanks, second, to the editors of the magazines in which the "New Poems" have appeared:

32 Poems: "What We Did That Year, and the Next"
Alabama Literary Review: "Love"
Hunger Mountain: "Order"
I-70 Review: "The Catastrophe of Next"
James Dickey Review: "Fame"; "Othello I, II, III"; "The Taming of the
    Shrew"; "Shylock and Romeo, the Only Two . . ."; "The
    Histories of Your Past and Future: Lesson One"; "For You at My
    Death"; "Slow Reads Out of Joint at the Fast-Food Joint"
Kestrel: "Here"; "The Two Rats of Art"
Literary Imagination: "Much Ado About Nothing"
Poetry Miscellany: "Overlay"; "The Ghost of Emily Dickinson at the
    Kroger Gas Station"
Shenandoah: "History of My Present"; "Fear . . . Not"

Snake Nation Review: "Dead Lift"; "The Art of Sex"
South Florida Poetry Journal: "Romeo and Juliet"; "The Two Gentlemen
    of Verona"
Southern Humanities Review: "Julius Caesar"
Southern Review: "Calyniction: Nihil Obstat"
Terrain.org: "A Midsummer Night's Dream"; "The Tick and the Tock"

And, finally, thanks to writer friends, living and gone, who over the
years helped many of the poems become better: Barri Armitage, Jim
Brooks, Rick Campbell, Doug Carlson, Robert Dana, Richard Eberhart,
Starkey Flythe, Jr., Lola Haskins, Brandy Kershner, Milton Kessler,
Robert Kroetsch, Jim Peterson, Edward Wilson, and Gene Zeiger,.

History of My Present
[New Poems]

I. *Order*

II. *Learning from Shakespeare*

III. *Overlay*

❖

from **The Last Magician** (1981)

Crafts

Loves

❖

from *Synchronized Swimming* (1984)

I *Learning to Live in America*

II *Fighting Death*

III *Whatever Light*

from *All These Lands You Call One Country* (1992)

I Attacking the *Pietà*

II from *Li Po and Tu Fu in America*

III The Blooming of Sentimentality

IV Remoldings

❖

from **There Is No Finished World** (2003)

Understand

Poems of This Size

Measures

Mortal Fathers and Daughters

Stone as Stone

❖

For all of them

History of My Present

[New Poems]

I: *Order*

Order

—for Rebecca

When I am gone, you must follow
this order: amongst the endless
shelves of books, the bones of my brain,
find the *Selected Poems of Pope*.
Lovely old Riverside edition,
classy pink-red paperback
supple and solidly bound,
glue fresh after fifty years,
or sixty. Riffle slowly. I
am there still, my right hand moving
on the ground beneath the maple
supporting my back as I lean,
nestle, reading in fall the heroic,
gentle, vicious, maudlin Pope. Find the one
hand-sized leaf, three-boled, brilliantly marbled
red with yellow veins, laid across
the Unfortunate Lady, tucked
firmly into the gutter seam,
weighted with my promise to save
the fleeting within the fleeting.

No, no red herrings this time—
Only straight-up gumption allowed.
You must trust me on the leaf's color,
long lost despite my quick waxing,
but the thing itself remains, rhymed
with, and clutched by, Pope's silken clamps.
Here is a life, and a life, and
a life. Not the same, but each the one.
Now . . . please: Save them. Save *it*. Please. Now.

What We Did That Year, and the Next

Balanced our new textbooks on their spines,
lowered each hard cover flat to our desks,
ran the heels of our hands down the gutters
listening for the hushed snap of excess
glue, the crackle of smoothing smooth paper,
knowing next we would take a clutch of pages
front and back and crease them down,
and then another brace of those printed wings
laid down, and then another, until only air
stood upright, our whole books now made
ready to be read, our palms and fingers tingling
and red from the working of malleability
into the hearts of our sheets that might be
blank for all we'd learned from them so far,
but then—then—we went on to our next
books, and our next, loading our desks
with pliant, longer-lived feathery tablets
we knew—because we trusted—would fill
our entire year with what could happen
nowhere else, since nothing else was bound
to turn our heads and eyes, to close our mouths
loaded with the fifth-grade crap we talked
ten other hours a day, and to send us reeling
down the cinder-block hallways of the real
imagination we were just learning lived
there—right there—in the words that wouldn't stop
if only we kept on opening.

Fame

For decades now, infants and tiny toddlers
have taken me in with their blank-seeming stares
while being ambled past in arms or on shoulders,
while being rolled past in strollers—
straining their necks to pull me
into their wordless worlds.

Now, decades on, I'm in states
I've never entered—flash of beard
in Boise, thin nose in Nebraska—
buzzing a thousand brains
with notions ungraspable:
turning a hermit toward politics,
quelling a rapist's thrust,
calming a deathbed tremor
with the ghost I've always been—
circling the world with silence.

Keep Talking

The thing worth saying once—say it again.
Learn to lead off with what little you know,
then fear no moment as the final one.

Electricity: her hand to your skin.
Say yes, say hand, say tongue, never say no—
that thing worth saying once . . . say it again.

Electricity: the chair you're born in.
When pain rides win and place, then pain rides show
to cant each moment toward the final one.

Yes, let's copy the *Yes* of Molly Bloom.
Yes, let's erase the alone of each *no*.
The thing once nearly said—say it this time.

One no be on — all born of *bone*. All bone
giving birth to and coming from marrow,
who's naming which moment the final one?

Lean, arch, lift, writhe, groan, swell, rise, ooze, spurt, moan.
We want the electric, always, fast *and* slow.
The one thing never said—say it again,
as if the final moment were the one.

New Delight

To succeed we must be kept from something,
need the barrier lingering between.
The clipping brings us to a stronger wing.

Spiritual carrots ride endless strings:
trim Jack's fat spouse—she's lusting for the lean;
imagined gnawing fuels the exiled king.

To majority minority will cling,
election's selection the frailest sheen.
To be freed we must be clamped by something.

The poem, painting, song—the golden ring
we miss and miss, our arms too short although we lean.
The botched creation holds the vital thing.

The held-still tension of the still-held spring,
the naked lover sighted through a screen—
swelling's truest antidote is swelling.

To invent we must be kept from something,
win the skirmish and not quite lose the fight.
There must be pressure, hard against the dream.
The grating brings us to a new delight.

Why They Are Good

> I recall, in sunlight,
> a strange angle of your leg
> as you lay naked on the ground.
> —The first good lines I ever wrote.

Because arousal gives back
poetry to passion, passion to poetry.
Because five *l*s are one
antidote to hell.
Because five *n*s make everything
grow, placing the whole tongue
against the palate and not
merely the leading tip, so useful
so often otherwise.
Because the syllables stepladder—
six, seven, eight—and the accents
swell—three, three, four—to meet
the arrival of nakedness.
Because the full force of the story
lies behind the three lines,
the twenty-one syllables left
to dream of adding the real
tongue, the real legs, the real.

The Two Rats of Art

The scratching of a pen
in a silent room
is a rat in the attic—
the flurry of scurryings,
the moments of silence—
as if the pursuit of food
and the finding.

At the heart of any memory
sits the rat of revision,
nibbling, gnawing, shifting
the shape to feed the self,
leaving the leavings
to dry and rot.

The Art of Sex

A woman's naked crotch hangs inches above me
on the coffeehouse wall, the hair, thighs, and belly
jaggedly snipped, leaving an impression
akin to that of a great chunk of broken pottery.
This photograph is art, but I still worry
women seeing me seated here will get the wrong idea.
I assume I could be arrested for moving my tongue
up and down and back and forth on the glass.
I'm pretty sure my fingers would also do,
especially if I kept it up until the police arrived.
What I'm wondering about is the air space
in front of the woman's body, in front of the art—
as in beachfront rights, underground rights, three-mile limits.
If I stood at the counter across the room, near the napkins and cream,
wiggling my fingers or tongue toward the photo,
would a crime be committed or imminent?
Suppose I were two feet away. Or one inch, never touching?
How can we think of such things? How can we not?
What if I stared for an hour? And also whistled or hummed?
Where is the line between art and life?
What is the distance?

Here

Here is Sappho, whose face we have never seen,
staring at the ocean. Here is the last Frenchman
to die—his name was not Napoleon—
in Napoleon's retreat from Russia,
this starved and frozen corpse not a whit
more dead nor less than our fathers.
Here is the bursting berry, and the cherry . . . but, no.
No to all these *here*s, which one after one
after one are *there*.
                    Here are my fingers, one after one
and together as well, on all of your skins:
the smooth but slightly tough foot-top,
your tendons raising furrows as you react;
the bristly almost-roughness of your calf
you might have shaven again had you known my hand
would return, though that slight resistance is
in fact another pleasure, prelude here to the here—
rising like a sudden swell in a trail, felt by legs
but invisible to eyes—of my hand approaching
the top of the calf, inside the knee, where
softness blooms as if it were a surprise
in the dark under the closed eyelid, and I
the child in that darkness being urged,
"Keep them closed, now, and hold out your hand."
And then, the sun and Shakespeare and the door to this room
ancient memories, I am here sliding your heart along,
just below—no, exactly within—your skin, as we move
those nearly eighteen inches upward, soft upon soft . . . .

For You at My Death

Either way, I could not do this then:

I'll be the one to sign off first,
joining the great dumb legions of Houdinis
swearing they would offer a sign;

or you will have gone, cutting me short
in the way of that great wooden crate
dropping from its corner perch
in the Tew Street garage—I was, what,
seven or eight?—to seal me flat beneath,
its vacuum leaving me with the first-ever breath
I could not take, even now those stymied lungs
a bright terror, though only seconds passed
before playmates lifted it to set me free.

Oh, but there would be no lifting,
only stones on the chests of poets
everywhere, the day you passed
and I was left behind to . . . .

Love

We are asked to get it right
the first time through, to walk through
thousands—thousands—of poppies,
to clutch one going past
then never reach out again.
This we call purity. This
we call faithful choosing. This
we call lost in love.

II *Learning from Shakespeare*

Romeo and Juliet

——for Tom

In Burlington, Vermont, the lovers glide
as dancers on the college green, shadowed
by the chapel and the sugar maples
Shakespeare—to his loss—could never write of.
Duck-duck-goosing around the dips and swirls
the full cast patterns in the dusk, R and J—
aren't they that familiar to us all?—
seem blithe and desperate at once. No play
here, even, only prologue to a darkness
houselights dimmed will make to mirror darkness
full by then on the grass sprung back, darkness
making ready inside—as if alive—
to fall on every step a world could take.

We did not enter the then-bright theater,
my cousin, his wife, and I. The offered dance,
suddenly not just the Capulet ball
foreshadowed, but the whole life, seemed enough.
We walked, they not quite thirty, I just past,
through the simpler night the city produced.
I neither saw nor dreamed the single hose
wedged through a back-seat window, heard no voice
failing to rise from a woman alone
in her sweet bitterness of chosen air.
I then heard no one entering the dark
garage to gather in the steeped, wrong flower.
I could not sense the world would offer up
its startling, constant promise quite so soon.

Slow Reads Out of Joint in the Fast-Food Joint

Passing behind me unseen, not peeking
carefully enough at my open tome,
she said, "I love to see people reading
the Good Book." and I felt no need, even
in a famous chain restaurant, to speak
my piece aloud as counter and support
to hers as she walked out from the building.
My book had one capital to her two—
this day she not knowing mine was *her* good
likewise, another mirror showing all
she could ever need—and one name to none,
Shakespeare to Good, Shakespeare to Book. So, she
could walk on happily, and I sit same
with her book feeding mine at every turn.

The Two Gentlemen of Verona

i

What they loved: love.
Whom they failed: lovers.

ii

The dollar bill   exhibits the Great Seal,
its floating eye   near a pyramid's peak
seeming always   the purest mystery—
child's terror,   adult's silent question—
its Latin tags   top- and bottom-heavy:
always watching,   they say, or *vigilant?*
Oh no, I say,   that eye is burning love
never sleeping,   loving all it sees,
carried abroad   by each woman, each man.
A loves *B, C*   loves *D* then *B. D's* left,
C fights with *A*   while *B* denounces *C.*
Easy enough,   this plotting out of life.
We have, at last,   just two things: the constant,
the inconstant.   We can each make our lists.
Shakespeare knew this.   Ophelia. Gertrude.
He hammered this.   Desdemona. Iago.
He laughed at this.   Henry the Fifth. Falstaff.
He wept at this.   Cordelia. King Lear.
Coin of the realm,   this flimsy scrim of love.
So contrary . . .   *go kindle fire with snow*
before you seek   to know the one of two,
the two of one   that spinning off will go.

Julius Caesar

The abuse of power is when it disjoins
Remorse from power . . .
                    Brutus, II, i

Little wonder this is—has been—the first
Shakespeare thrust at our keen pubescent horde,
this, the truly American message:
before honor and laughter, aging and loss,
even before love, we show them power:
the full corruption, the partial—the way
these two are the only ways.
                              "Greek to me,"
one murderer crowed of an innocent's words—
as if failure to understand were virtue,
suspicion a sign of wisdom,
violence the single translatable word.

We are a practical lot, we grownups,
in teaching and parenting.
                              Our fat dogs,
History and Culture, floppily wag
from the tails of impatience and ego.
Community's portrait is smeared. Lacking
the will to turn from a cracked mirror,
we lick or own genitals and call it love.

And yet, small suns peek through. The women,
their time onstage far too brief before death,
afford us chill glimpses of sanity:
Portia with her single scene, seeking
In vain to ease and aid the floundering
Brutus, then swallowing fiery coals,
believing only the most perverse demise
could squelch the pain of traitors and their greed.

Lone Calpurnia, her nightmares of death
and chaos Caesar's only path to life,
simply dissolves in the spreading acid
poured by men whose shadows, even, weigh more
than an honest woman's heart.
                                        No winners
emerge—one more plus for our cynical
youth who know that adult's adult, period.

Seers reviled, liars embraced, poets mocked—
this realm, you would think, we'd banish
like a pox come knocking and wailing at our shores.
Oh no. In our desperate, clutching dreams,
believing we might convert by bad example,
we feed the empty, thoughtless stomachs of our minds.

Yet all this we keep on paper only,
the staging of *Caesar* all but forbidden
on the boards that support a thousand *Our Towns*,
endless supplies of arsenic and lace,
star-crossed lovers, and midsummer nights—
for these have humor, however grim or sad;
for these have love good enough to go bad.
Caesar laughs not, neither through cynic,
fool, nor underling. *Caesar* melts not, burns
only for steely tempering to ice:

          "Alas, my lord,
          Your wisdom is consumed in confidence."

          "Cry 'Havoc,' and let slip the dogs of war."

          "You have some sick offense within your mind."

→

So we pretend the children could not bear
these words from the vibrant mouths of others,
force them to listen in their silent minds.
We pretend irony lives, though it doesn't
for hungry Cassius at the bloody trough:

> "Stoop, then, and wash. How many ages hence
> Shall this our lofty scene be acted over
> In states unborn and accents yet unknown!"

The future sees the truth of the past—far
less brutal than the past dicing for the future—
but nowhere does present read present,
nowhere the hand without knife, the voice
"so firm it cannot be seduced," the babes
whose skins do not go red and sere.

The Taming of The Shrew

Faith, as you say, there's small choice in rotten apples.
— Hortensio to Grumio, I, i

Can we forgive the one who murders, who
betrays? Does motive matter? Circumstance?
Hunger? Beating scars? Being named a shrew?

Doug Pastorchik was poor—his house, one glance
told me when we wandered in from playing,
a dirty my mother would not allow.

Doug's older brother—thirteen to our nine?—
gave me my first sight of a cig pack rolled
in a T-shirt sleeve, eyed me a small sign
I take now to have meant embarrassment,
took then as threat or sneer, an instant grasping
tight my fear. We could not break the distance frame.

There was dogshit on the rug. I can't recall his name.

Much Ado About Nothing

Which cover lightly, gentle earth!
—Ben Jonson

—Fargo, North Dakota: Now, just four more
Syllables for the lead-off ten-count line,
Datelined—that's right—Fargo, North Dakota.

Now, after this line, just ten more to go
Were this a sonnet, Shakespeare's strength. It's not.

Just self-analysis, mirror sucking,
As when I studied my eyes through the days
Following my daughter's death, following
The world's attempts to fit back into my brain
As if one grew from two, *a* from *b*, and all
The maps forgot they'd be out of business
Without her there (read *here*) to name them, she
The source of places and reasons, she
The all that was not, ever, nothing.

Othello I, II, III

I

> *. . . hell and night*
> *Must bring this monstrous birth to light.*
> —Iago

Perfect evil earns respect
for that single moment we marvel
at anything beyond our doing;
then we hate, and then we hate
for being forced to hate—
which makes us, however faintly,
companions to the monstrous.

II

> *Pathetic power corrupts pathetically.*

Trust without wariness is foolish.
This fact is irredeemably sad—
like all abstract assertions, even the true.

III

> *They are all but stomachs, and we all but food;*
> *They eat us hungrily, and when they are full*
> *They belch us.*
> Emilia to Desdemona

They . . . They . . . they . . . They . . . .
Oh, Emilia . . . Oh, Desdemona.
Your play . . . Your play.

Shylock and Romeo, the Only Two . . .

. . . who have left the stage and entered the world
via dictionary definition,
whose huge energies of greed and passion
earned them front-row dictionary places,
their names no longer names nor instances
but—trochaic, dactylic—the bare, forked
things themselves. Be not a Shylock. Perhaps
be not a Romeo—"philanderer"
no, but "ardent lover" yes—yet these two
are one as well as two, while a Shylock's
a Shylock only: bloodthirsty, fated
to a bottommost circle, yet famous.

A Midsummer Night's Dream

—for Aimee

Oberon: *Fetch me this herb; and be thou here again*
Ere the leviathan can swim a league.

Puck: *I'll put a girdle round about the earth*
In forty minutes.

Suppose the world were only Puck—
absent all royals and lesser nobles,
absent fools and fairies,
filled by the good heart so good
even its trickery is love and playfulness,
the scheming just innocent dreaming of joy.

But there is no summer, no night, no dream—
a winter's afternoon, this tale, and true:
a young friend in the part cannot dissolve
the magical line so cannily wrought,
so there she is, before me always,
even when silent and out of sight.

She could cause love, *this* Puck, to fly
via the purple flower's juice, laid in any eye
to save a life or mock it forcefully;
she did this with a forty-minute flight
around the Earth, mocking its vastness
to enthrall her school friends, their smugness.

If the same chills rise from Puck's sweet amends
as from sagging Lear's quintuple *nevers*,
where now in this thousand-and-more-page world

➜

do we find ourselves—our footing, our hearts?
Dear Aimee, bosom friend of my daughter,
outshining history and magic seems
so right for you, so nearly right for us.

III *Overlay*

The Ghost of Emily Dickinson (1830–1886) at the Kroger Gas Station

I always go for absolutely full,
Re-click the pump past auto-shutdown
To the, supposedly, overflow point.
Today I pocketed my frail receipt,
Headed home, pulled out the glassine slip,
Saw the final count: 18.86.
Without my calling her back she had come,
Unsensed by anyone, not even me—
The one who sees her so often, the one
Whose dream is to enter her lovely brain,
The astonishing electric flowing
Born in, and from, this world that was her bourne.

The First

Not many have
I loved—not so
many that I've lost
the space for each
where each began.

So few lives means
so few deaths—means,
however, one
for each. A match.

And now the first
is gone, is not
within the realm
of the *maybe*,
the *if*, a touch.

So fully
empty the space.

Dead Lift

—for Mary Ann Coleman, poet (1928-2002)

I find they have left your body elsewhere
when I enter the bright and spare
Episcopal space, so my final sight of you
becomes one I cannot recall: out through
some store window as you passed on the street?
Your photo in the paper? Crackling sheet
music slips from the organist's hands, delaying
the next set of your cherished notes to ring
these ears—these everyone's, these mine.

> *dead lift*: direct lifting without
> any mechanical assistance,
> as of a dead weight

Pallbearers show us our griefs perfected:
"Look, we raise this form dissected
six ways to an airy thinness all can suffer
smoothly, six mirrors of Mary Ann, her
heart six units of ash within this box."
We would grip them ourselves, the shock
disbursed by lightness thrilling our forearms, except
you are not here: the bare nave and transept
leave us lifting a wail, a whine.

> *dead lift*: a type of exercise
> in which a person lifts a barbell
> off the floor, stands up straight,
> and holds the weight hanging
> downward at arm's length

→

I know you knew this would be next, or soon,
this pen with iron point fused to our fist, this loon
call from the weird, blank lake we always try to swim—
our writing hands the metronome of mind, the grim
support to which huge Atlas lent his body whole.
The pen buckles, buckets of thought and death on its pole.

> *dead lift*: [archaic] a difficult task
> requiring all one's power.

I bear nothing to what the front row carries—
your granddaughter up to read your poems as if on her knees,
your grandson managing the squirming of his chattering daughter.
Bless them for not shushing her, or walking her out for water.
All the sounds and voices are called for here;
unless we speak, we neither stay nor steer.

Poet Editing Death

In those earliest years I chose the line
measuring the softest skin I knew, there
along the crease of her uppermost thigh,
at the edge of the pubic hair spreading
in toward her other forms of softness.

Next I liked works of further devotion,
love that knew lust but peered beyond its wall.
Also, soon, the songs of new life grabbed me:
babies in bloody emergence, toddlers
on the grass or beach, first words on the air.

I saw where all this was going, but still
I made my chilled-heart choices, my holdings,
cuts, and perfectings: "Drop *this*, polish *that*."
There was no stopping my love for the art
that told me what I loved, what never stopped.

Poems of fucking came to embarrass me,
but only across those few brief years
I pretended youth gone, pretended aging.
I sought tryst and *triste* for opposing
pages, for lovers and dying parents.

Past fifty I started to think—poor boy—
finding thought could bring back sex, banish death,
run St. Elmo's fire up every mast;
too old then to believe I was older,
old enough to write the previous line.

One thing equals one poem—then move on:
Her astonishing ass, naked above me
as we climb the ladder to the loft.
My father in a room I never saw,

his last breaths at 3 a.m., my birth time.
My first child in her bassinet, lying
asleep since the trip from the hospital—
her tininess terrifying, the ten
fingers of her hands fingers of my hand
curling, stretching, editing death away.

Calyniction: *nihil obstat*

Again they have leapt from the fence to stun me,
moonflowers as Superman, entering
nature's booth as nondescript vines, leaving
the neighbors' yard for mine and blowing up
the dark with their white-hot discs—shaming lilacs,
roses, any other flower you could name.
My mother is one week dead. The real moon
glints with astonishing softness atop
the neighbors' brick chimney, whose burnished steel
top-shield broadcasts the local heavens' news.
And as if there could never be enough
to ponder and absorb, a strange creature
begins to flit among the lit blossoms:
hummingbird it seems at first, all whirring
plus proboscis—but no, not at night, and not
with this insect's body, these too-large wings
flaring like a dragonfly's signature.
I want more light for study, more sight
for certainty, but dare not go back
inside, knowing only flowers would remain
at my return. And so they would: the flier
flees momently, now two beings and none—
and in another glittering story,
in just such stretch of time, some god made up some world.

Calyniction — moonflower; *nihil obstat* [Latin, nothing obstructs]. 1. In the Roman Catholic Church, a printed phrase, followed by the name of an officially appointed censor, indicating that the publication carrying the phrase has been examined and judged free of doctrinal or moral error. 2. Any official indication of non-opposition.

Fear . . . Not

In truth, fear the chronic, not the acute—
for if we burn we burn at worst a day.
The acute is fiery red, the chronic gray.

To fade and rot, drifting down an endless chute,
slathers arctic night on brightest day—
for sure, fear the chronic, not the acute.

A day without touch leaves another day;
hands crippled or gone will render skin moot.
Fucking is fiery red, chastity gray.

The wrench, the twist, the gash, the sledge of brute
action tears, splits, or flattens flesh away,
then heals. In pain's game, chronic flogs acute.

Eternity blathers on, chokes today
with golden mist disguising tarnished loot—
Earth is hot-wire red, heaven ashen gray.

Stretch of mind is long, body's reach minute.
Buck up: in time's fat mouth we *will* be prey,
but one clean crunch—not chronic, just acute.
Think red, sing red, dream red. At bay the gray.

Overlay

I was tired of the shouting and the celery,
the ignitions and navels and telephones.
I moved to a country where everything happened abstractly.

I had heard about this place in some translated poems:
a country filled with suffering and death and hope
and politics and minds to ponder them constantly.

But I was shocked by the new place, which proved to have
      many actual things;
mating turtles, good cheap bread, homeless four-year-olds
      walking the streets,
a museum filled with gold objects worth more than all
      the governments of South America,
and clouds that offered fog four months per year, though never rain.

I learned that the translators were not there,
but back in my own country amid sofas and taxis and loud music
and slaughtered chickens, wishing for the misery and change
this other country's poets might provide by turning
dirty shoes to sorrow, potatoes to faith,
loud music to notes that would lay over ours—
doubling our worlds or canceling them out.

The Tick and The Tock

The Tick

You don't know if the mark on your skin is new
because you can't tell if it has legs. If, when
you magnify the mark, it does, then you have to
get it out. My mother used to do that with a lit
cigarette by bringing it close enough to burn
my thin skin, and when the legs backed off
she would kill them. Sometimes the pain from
the ashes would wake me. Sometimes I'd dream
red eyes circling my bed, wolves around a tent.

They ask that about a poem—does it have legs?
And if, when you look closely, it does, you'd
best get it all down because if you don't you
Can come down with what looks like flu but, unlike
flu, will last the rest of your life. Odd, I'd say,
that you never think how those legs emerged,
clinging to a slim blade of swaying grass
at the side of some trail, and how only by chance
did you pass by and sweep them away.

The Tock

You know the mark on your skin is old
because every day it is new at dawn, then
through the hours magnifies, darkens, outs
the loss—yesterday's, tomorrow's—close
against your flesh like tiny legs, circling.
My lover used to wake me, her eyes the lit
cigarettes of my dreams, burning and red
with the closeness we needed . . .feared . . .
but craved, whether wolf or angel.

They ask that about love—can it stand
and keep moving, have the full body
the heart needs for the rest of your life?
Can a heart have legs, or must it settle
only for itself, for always running on
in place—in those ones, tens, hundreds,
schmundreds—until nothing can hold
it back, unless it holds itself back—
holds back, rests, then becomes nothing?

The Catastrophe of Next

Suppose this were my Greek anthology,
my single piece surviving
the catastrophe of next.
What should it . . . ?

Assertive to provoke.
Shadowy to mystify.
Erotic to rouse.
Gentle to calm.

Mud crumbling.
Stone standing.
Resonance.
Chill.
Heat.
Ink.
On.
O.

The Histories of Your Past and Future: Lesson 1

The past had a past it was trying to overcome,
one about which it believed improvements had been made;
the future looks back your way with amazement, hatred,
berating your arrogance, your dumb and fumbling ways.

History of My Present

One could do worse than march toward posterity
sandwiched by *gardens* and *garfish*—
the fate of the only U.S. president
to have a direct descendant
who became a fifth-grade teacher
who had me as one of her students.

This isn't a test, but list three key events
from the Garfield term of office.
Also its length. How about *one* event?
Or maybe the man's first name?
Take as long as you need—
something that he didn't get.

Sexy Miss Garfield, triple-great-grandchild
controlling our daily recess scene,
belting the shit from a softball
kicking the shit from a kickball
nailing the whole class in dodgeball
and always her car top down.

Twentieth president almost by mistake—
drafted to break a Republican stalemate—
James earned the victor's spoils but dumped them
to clear the decks on a rotten ship of state:
Civil Service, thy name is Garfield.
(That's one. You want to switch to Lincoln?)

Marlene she was, blond and twenty-three,
picking up Louie and me—total years, twenty—
in her bright-yellow Ford for a Popsicle run
after school, her hair blowing wild in my face.
What was she thinking, in 1958? What were *we*?
Innocence A, Innocence B and C.

Barton's Red Cross emerged during Garfield's reign,
and Booker T.'s Tuskegee Institute,
but neither through his signature,
though some will say—for instance, *moi*—
he gave his time, however brief, a certain air,
this man who shunned the Credit Mobilier.

I was ten. My pubes were hairless, our town was small.
What did I know of sexual women?
But for thirteen years my life was lived with women
teachers, and only one—Miss Garfield—burns
now when I try to trace the fires back
into the pit still pulsing, bright and dark.

Well, 'twas *Senator* Garfield battled Credit Mobilier
(such a lovely phrase for evil, let's say it twice),
refusing the railroad gang's proffered grease,
so still we've only one grand moment—
but what surprise here when you recollect,
as I asked up front, his length of term in office?

No, she never touched me, and of course
I never her. It was not like that, though what it was
I could not say. (I mean, I do not know.)
Do senses of power and importance carry down
through families more strongly than otherwise?
Do fears of early death? Was anything James Marlene?

Four years living, three and a half dying.
The plot's too good for truth; this poem must be fiction.
The next year Marlene disappeared, moved on
as the younger ones often did, but I wondered . . . .
Then, I dreamed she could not teach without me
in the room. Now I wonder, was she asked to leave?

→

The president's killer was unemployed,
denied his purchased inch of public trough,
herded into failure by a test of competence.
Garfield's job became suffering the bullet
lodged against his spine, the draining away
through pain of his one promise: honesty.

I'd like to say I dreamed Miss Garfield
ran off with Charles Guiteau—you know,
John Wilkes Booth, Lee Harvey Oswald—
but I want this story to come around true:
I do not know what happened to Guiteau;
if I dreamed of Marlene, I've forgotten how.

The Star Route scandal had really set James off—
U. S. Mail delivery roads, sold for contractor kickbacks.
He'd see the Civil War brew and begin
from the Ohio Senate, watched it blow up and bleed
as a Union officer, watched it die and fester
from the U.S. House. He'd brook no more division.

March 4th through July 1st, 1881—
those were the president's days on his feet.
Alexander Graham Bell searched for the slug
with a homemade electrical probe. In vain.
July 2nd through September 19th—Garfield's days
for lying-in till death. He was fifty.

I think I scarcely recall her face.
Her hair, its color and fall, I still believe in.
And the shape of her hips under the fitted skirts
she wore while somehow still outrunning us all
on the base paths. The great, slow arcs of her arms
sweeping her notes on the board for emphasis:
Learn this. Learn *this*. Remember.

from

The Last Magician

(1981)

Crafts

Embroidery

Nothing less than painting by thread—
needling hawks to cover a cowboy's chest,
nightingales for a regal cloak,
daisies for the pillow of a child.

Like the best of lovers,
the threads interweave and overlay
but cannot be fused on any palette—
each bright line unique
as the music of broid.

Smith

I go to church on the rims of carriage wheels,
into the chest on the scalpel.
I am hinged and latched to every village home,
hammered deep into my own hammer.

Call me farrier on a cloudy day
and I just might split your skull—
better call the poet a printer's devil.
If the sun is right, I'll spare you, sit you down
while I forge a Swedish lock and key.

What non-living things recreate themselves?
Tools. Tools the others must have to begin.
What can I do that lovers only dream?
Fuse two things into one, forever.
Would you turn your back on me?
Go then. But remember: the world is mounted
on the rainbow of firing iron—from black
to palest yellow, through blues and reds to blazing white—
and only I can read the shade
between bend and break, shape and ruin.

Quilts

One woman wept, they say,
when a peddler reached her cabin
with no new patterns to sell.

Irish Chain, Persian Pear, Rose of Tennessee

I still make my bed with *Kansas Troubles*—
I was only five when Mother said,
"Twelve you must have in your hope chest, before
the Bridal Quilt, and that before you'll wed."
First my stitches tried to mirror hers,
our hands touching as we worked.
At night she plucked mine out
to keep her project whole.
Next came simple sewings: double lines
and scallops on my own crazy quilt.

Bear Track, Turkey Track, Beauty of Kaintuck

Some days, when Tommy and Jimmy ran outside
shouting off the chickens, I thought
I'd stretched myself across that frame, waiting
for the womenfolk to pad and quilt and bind me.
Yet with all the years of work,
when the time came Joseph had to wait
seven months while I finished Jacob's Tears.
The Bridal must be perfect, Mother warned.
A broken thread, a crop gone bad;
a twisted stitch, a baby dead.

→

Wreath of Grapes, Flying Swallows, Pomegranate Tree

Sometimes our life is no more than the names we give:
Joseph moved us to Missouri,
And the women loved my *Jacob's Tears*—
but they knew it as *The Slave Chain*.
In the Texas flatland winds, *Texas Tears*
lay across the bed, and after the last move
we slept warm beneath *The Road to Kansas*.
That was many droughts and storms ago.
The colors still blaze enough to shame
a Puritan, and not a seam has given way.
Joseph is gone, but even coldest nights
my *Kansas Troubles* brings me through till dawn.

Potter

The potter's always praying over his kiln.

Winters of smearing hot water
on frozen clay in my shed
have deadened the nerves in my fingers.
Spinning earth between my hands
has worn my fingerprints away.

My recurring dream is a common thing:
to finish some work and claim it as my own.
But I wake to the heating or cooling kiln,
cursed by an art beyond my control.
Fire is a fickle and vicious editor.

Will these words explode or melt beneath my hands?
Dear God, I touch my wife in the night
and cannot feel her skin.
I could kill her, throw myself
into some new life, never be traced.

Whittler to His Lover

I began whittling this branch
as the first of a hundred pegs
for a new old-fashioned cabinet.

Something scared me off,
kept me carving
down to this brown bead
I ask you to wear
for what we can and cannot do.

Explaining Glassblowing to a Glassblower

Breath makes another world here.
The apprentice carries a gather of glass
on the blowpipe to the gaffer's bench,
then rolls the molten glob
on the cold steel plate of the marver
to form a rubbery skin. The gaffer blows the piece.
His helper presses the hot metal rod
(the ponty) against the glass,
the gaffer scissors the glass from the pipe.
Heatings at the Glory Hole allow the detail-work;
cooling in the lehr saves the finished piece.

Art is sometimes defined as magic,
magic as the strange, and the strange
as no more than a sound. Finding the right man,
we could say *sponge, bucket, scrub*—
and his skin would prickle
at the world he had found.
We could laugh him off and go on cleaning,
but know less than this man who saw
the new and luminous in our work.

Scrimshaw

There are some that make their mark
out on the water with a long stroke,
harpoon heaved from behind the shoulder,
twisting through the blubber.
I hold back, wait for bone.

I look hard around, then knife it all—
even the rigging—in close black lines
on the tooth between my knees.
A man who's lost his foot
deserves to stay away
from flying ropes and trying oil,
but this work's more than fair—
no whale's ever stayed on his own bones,
nor kept a ship beside him.

Watch the flames dance like flukes
in your lamp. No matter how big
the well, how many barrels you bought,
you go dry. And I pitch there on the mantel,
dark lines in the dark, sounding strong.

Carpenter: Of His Pleasures

The second finest thing is handing them the wood
to let them wonder at the smoothness
that makes them feel they could prod
their thumbs into the grain as into flesh.
Eleven sandings to get that sheen
before the varnishing.
                    Taking the twelfth paper,
sanding to remove what I first discern
by touch, then by trusting guess alone—
and after that work, handing it back again,
knowing they'll sense no difference—
that is the finest thing.

State Craft Fair: Berea, Kentucky

Between the pines dozens of quilts
flap heavily on lines, out of place
like the wash of some flamboyant hermit.
This is a place to commit suicide—
at every step you are amazed and beaten down
by some excellence.
                              Here is cloth,
fresh as bread from its clattering loom.
Here are stoneware plates
shining with geese you'll never lose to Canada.
And always at your feet,
cut-rate bowls and mugs in crates—
even failure can be beautiful and watertight.

That largest crowd surrounds the Winslow boys.
Henry plays the newest mandolin
while Samuel works beside him on the next,
sanding the frets and laying them on.
Nothing goes wrong. The people stare
as if they had walked into a womb.

Old Musician, Tuscaloosa, 1859

He could have picked clean and true
on stretched threads of corn silk.
He was the singer you hear
in your head when you know
the right sadness could save your life.

They came in the night
and dragged him to the barn,
axed his fingers on the anvil,
sliced off his tongue.

Five weeks later he climbed
from the bed, lifted a mash jug
between his wrists, walked out
to set it on the porch rail.
Bending forward he puffed, slow and resonant,
the day's first song over the pines.

The World's Largest Poet Visits Rural Idaho

His 300 pounds on his 6-11 frame
will not fit into the dean's VW
waiting at the bus station. He must wait again
while a 40-mile round trip brings another car.

At the Pine Tree Motel the world's largest poet
piles baggage on the underlength bed,
naps on blankets on the tile floor.

That evening, a low table his only podium,
he ducks and squints to read his poems.

Both he and his hosts are aware of all this.
They have him for the glaciers and wild birds
that spring from his giant fingers.
He's there because the battered humming
in his head will not stop.

To an Ex-Student on Learning She Is a World-Class Gymnast

—for Ann Woods

What routines you must have mounted
in Mycenae and Greece
while the rest of us studied texts
in our windowless room:
your chalked palms know
they can vault the Cretan bull's horns,
your spine curling down
to the rough, frothing beam of his back.
In the Test of the Bow, you dance
across the axe-helves, beggaring
even the hero's threaded shot.
You sit with a hand on Homer's thigh
as that night's *Odyssey* becomes itself.
As the poet fights
the strange and familiar magic of his brain,
your touch reminds him
the tongue is first a muscle.
Your silent sprung flights and twistings show
what the body of his song can be.

On Being Named Literary Executor in the Event of Your Death

Given a stone-filled box
marked "feathers," one's hands would drop
toward the floor, fighting to grip
what seems a jolt of magic.

Arriving with bills and casual notes,
your letter asks me to enter
your poems as guardian, judge, prophet.
I must finish you,
give the world the version it deserves.
Should the blossom be rose or mimosa?
Should the food be smilax or corn?
There can be no mistake. Even nightmare
Must be perfected, and blank spaces measured.

No one could hold this box without dying
into it: giving himself to falling,
as if some tired goddess had begged him
to rise and sustain the Earth.

Baptism for the Dead

The Mormon Church urges members
To trace their ancestry back at
Least four generations in search
of photographs of relatives who
were never baptized into the faith.
These can then be saved by performing
a baptism for the dead.

I   THE ANGEL MORONI

A person's face shall be his soul.
This one invention shall be God's instrument.
These glass plates shall have the weight of stone.

II   ESTELLA MANWARING BROCKBANK

I'm on the right, not quite touching mother.
I recall Mr. Anderson first
in Jacob Smith's yard. At our place
he put Jane and Carrie's elbows
on Mother's lap, and me to the side.
That's why I looked at the camera
instead of praying. Mother scolded me later.
The picture man said he'd never seen
anything so white as those three gowns.
Two years after the picture, when I was eleven,
a landslide killed my sisters in Colorado.
That was seventy-four years ago.
When Mr. Francis found the negatives
in that Springville basement—thousands—
word spread there'd be many we could save.
Mr. Francis had Salt Lake City
pounding on his door. Three men broke in,

→

smashed dozens of plates
searching the dark faces for their kin.
Isn't Mother's face as bright as her medallion
in the light, there on the right side?
Carrie was four, Jane was six.
I touched their small faces
in the tabernacle, and the elders touched them.
I swear Mother's face was brighter afterwards,
and the angel Moroni was in the air.

III   THE KEEPER OF THE PLATES

Without the names others bring,
the faces I make are nothing.
I've printed hundreds of folks
still trapped in my studio.
Look at these ten under the trees—
only three have been named.
Sometimes I wish I could send the others back—
white leaves and white grass around them,
black hands in their laps,
white eyes glowing with an unknown chance for grace.

Virginia Woolf

1882-1941

Everything in your life led here.

The threads you saw connecting
all others with yourself were real,
but did not stop there as you thought.
Those wiry silks bored on through
the hearts of those you knew and cared for,
curved and turned to bring themselves
sinewing to this March and wartime bank.

Waves always charged and whipped your senses,
waves of color, sound, scent, beauty,
waves in folds of a green silk dress.
You were the diamond shore of your world,
all waves roaring into you—
waves of blood, friendship, politics, madness—
then refracted out purified to water,
always running, pure but uncontrolled,
here to the River Ouse.

You were your own glacier.
through fifty-nine years the bone splinters,
blue petals, oak trees of your life
inched toward this stream's melting power.
Then, as your rock-weighted body
settled in, nature's rules collapsed:
when you reached bottom
your flesh and stones became water, while
the stream became the glacier
and your body would not move
from its ring of glowing ice
in a hundred thousand years.

Self-Destructing Poem

Boiling down
is for maple syrup
whale blubber
the cabbage of song

The Earth
is not something
buried within a tree
You are not
flesh melting to oil
The pot holding this
black vegetable
must froth and boil
over

The Last Magician

We remember from childhood three magicians:

the one cutting women in half
driving swords through midgets in boxes
making grown elephants disappear;

the one with cards and coins
coming and going,
in at your nose
out from his ear,
growing in number
or changing faces
at a wink
or the rub of a palm;

the one dropped from an ocean pier,
manacled, cemented, gagged
as he disappeared, absolutely gone
for ninety seconds, then bobbed back
toward the leaning crowd,
sputtering and free.

The machinery we come to accept,
the gifted muscles we admire
yet sometimes catch in their act.
But this Houdini, taking weights on his pale body,
dropping to perform on a stage
we can barely imagine,
remains.

Loves

Love: A Definition

He remembers a room
wind blew across, a room
where books and silence held
and he expected nothing.

He remembers a door
swung open in the house
somewhere far below, and

he recalls that then the pitch
of breeze through his singing window
was ever so slightly raised.

The Lovers Visit the Museum

A small room is marked "Nature's Ghosts":
the white shapes are like favorite clothes
mistakenly bleached, their familiarity lost
in disquieting blankness.
The red eyes of the fawn show
so strongly that its pale body,
Cheshire, almost disappears.
The albino brown bat is pinned under glass,
wings like peeled and drying human skin;
his arms, fingers, legs, and tail
glow orange, his teeth are translucent.
If he were alive, we could watch
the blood flowing through his body.
If we could set him loose in the night
darkness would shine through
as if he were scarcely there..

Our hands press together to stop
whatever has been draining away.
How much of ourselves can we lose
before we surrender,
how much must we lose to know
we are now some other thing?

Falling in Love at Forty

One needs it more now.
Adolescence has so much else
to keep itself feeling young.

Yukio Mishima,
approaching middle age,
wrote in his diary
"Today I have learned to move
a new abdominal muscle."

Perhaps I must ask
no more nor less than this:
that the backs of my hands
become suddenly strange,
that I may study them
as my palms enclose your face,
that the veins of what was always mine
somehow come back to me again.

Softening the World by Your Body

Knead the dough until it is ear lobe consistency.
—pie crust recipe, *Deaf Smith Country Cookbook*

I roll each politician between my palms
until he changes from my elbow
to the inside of your wrist: rough, flaking skin
to a cool white untouched by sun.

I bake the borders of every country
until they are the two-inch valley
from the base of your spine
down into the cleft of your buttocks—
a petal-soft mystery whose only secret
is that no beauty can fight against itself.

I touch this warm new earth to my lips
to prove it is the hollow of your neck
just above the clavicle—a planet whose windpipe
and vocal cords are so near the surface,
we need only listen to her breath and the words
she makes, and she might be ours forever.

The Butcher's Daughter to Her Lover

—for Janet

Swinging on the meat hooks after school,
Father yelling when I kicked the hanging sides.
Barrels of guts and bones in the walkway
between shop and house, cats and flies swarming—
when I'd pass too near the barrels
the cats would follow me to the dusty yard
licking my ankles and the tops of my feet.
Mother did all the work—sawing, slicing,
weighing—while father sat all day
as if he'd just dropped down to rest.

If I let you touch me now, you must promise
not to sink into a chair, never to rise.
You must not fall apart
in scraps of red and white.

The Ugly Stepsisters

We hobble blind through the world—alive.
What would you do to be touched by the prince?
Toss you own toes under the bed
before he entered, sit with your back turned coyly
to slide your bloody foot into the slipper?
What would you give for that ride beside him?—
the parading moment with the castle in sight
before those pigeons cried you down:
"Look, the right bride sits at home!"
Even after the thing you loved was given,
once more, to the beautiful, would you limp and crawl
to the church, dreaming of one more chance?
When those damned pigeons gouged your eye
but left you with one to watch the wedding,
when you knew they would be waiting after in the trees,
would you leave the church to walk home, knowing
you were right?
                    Beauty loses nothing when it pays court
to ugliness. We cried when we saw how she fixed our hair—
what could we do but ask for more?
In some far corner of the Earth, beside her skin
old blood stains the deepest recess of the slipper.
We feel it still, that moment when we made it fit.

Marriage

Would you rot for me if I asked?
Most of it would be easy—like trees
quiet there side by side, almost touching,
tending to look the same year after year.

The surprise would come from the inside,
working outward ring by ring
in a sad race from pith to cortex.

The question would be who cracks first
in what gale, spattering at the break point
into spongy pieces as shocking
as a house you could squeeze in your fingers.

The final mystery would occur
when one, falling, strikes the other:
could the stronger stand,
witness the explosion against itself?
Or will the falling one dive through
the softening core, Baucis and Philemon
disintegrating like planes in collision?

These are my wedding proposals.

The Famous Waving Girl

Florence Martus, 1843-1908

Forty-four years you stood on the cliff
before your island home, waving
a white handkerchief to every ship
in or out of Savannah's harbor.

Some sailors leered through the spyglass
at a young girl, years later laughed at an old woman.
Most dreamed of your swaying silhouette—
made you the mother in a Bristol graveyard,
the lover on a Portsmouth widow's walk,
the wife never found on any shore.

You began with a child's gesture:
setting down *Wuthering Heights*, raising an arm
to match your white cloth against the sails.
Young men waved back—the connection made.
Frequent returns to the cliff became
constant vigils at the bedroom window,
became the drawer of kerchiefs washed by hand,
ironed, piled flat for uncreased fluttering.

Early on you dreamed of surrender,
daring your coquettish scarf to fall
upon the passing decks below.
Later came the hope for escape,
the white flag of desperation.
They shouted, they furled and unfurled banners,
their signal-fires reddened the sea's black,
but on they sailed for half a century.

The white handkerchief. At the end,
the last bleached leaf of the island's only tree,
your own bones waving in your hand.

In Raney's Cavern

The young tour guide extends a green-sleeved arm
toward a light switch on the rock face.
As her hand flips the switch she stops talking
for the first time since we lunged
through the turnstiles and down beneath Raney's Mountain.
She lets us feel it alone for ten or twenty seconds:
pressing our faces, loosening our children's fingers,
trying to tip us over the iron rail we clutch.
I cannot tell if I have blinked.

"For most of you, this is your first time
in absolute darkness. Left here for several hours,
many of you would go mad." Her programmed voice,
accented, lifted, and lowered in all the wrong places,
is suddenly beautiful. Some story of Indians,
smugglers, and Civil War deserters—men who used this dark
to shape a life impossible above.
Her words blur toward music, coming at me
from every side. Even the toddlers are silent.
My sense of balance gone, I could die here
but for the singing of this girl—whose thoughts as she sings
must be with hamburgers, with Friday nights
roaring down Raney's Mountain in her boyfriend's Chevrolet.

Migration

To this small hill in Mexico
comes every Monarch butterfly alive.
You can lie on the grass and be covered
with hundreds of bright and weightless bodies.
From a short distance off, you will appear
as a shimmering black and orange angel
burning against the hillside. You can think
how the rest of the world is empty
now of this beauty which buries you here.
It will leave for fifty weeks,
but will return in different bodies
to this same place, and will light upon you
if you are here. Can you refuse these rests,
these hair-like legs brushing you until it seems
they could lift your skin into the sky?

Condition: Pachyderm

1. ELEPHANT EARLY MORNING

Waking, I find the elephants
everywhere performing
tasks thought before to be human.

My first vision—
a well-tuskered rogue
in green coveralls
straddling the driver's seat
atop a yellow snowplow—
strikes me just so: a vision.
Short sleep, early winter ground-fog,
music blare as I drive the empty streets—
all things join to explain all things.

2. SHORT-ORDER ELEPHANT

The glare of the 7 a.m. diner
explodes evasions:
behind the counter
a pleasantly wrinkled two-ton cow
stands gracefully with rocky-round feet
resting on the countertop.
She trumpets to a drowsy human customer,
his head hanging,
staring at his coffee cup
flanked by giant feet.

Through the order window
a young bull can be seen
flashing about the grill.
His trunk curls the spatula
swirling and chopping scrambled eggs,
a snowy chef's hat
balances on his great skull.
Stomach deadened, I burst the doorway
running to my car . . . race off.

3. ELEPHANT GRACE

My car skids down icy streets,
soon plows two-foot drifts of country roads.
Miles from the city, heart slowed,
I brake at a sudden roadside scene:
on a fire-pond beside a rotted barn
two yearling cows skate with awesome grace:
hind legs flow on blades on heavy ice,
front legs wave with Olympic medal form,
trunks swing in perfect rhythm.

Hands shaking, car clumsy with snow,
again I flee.

→

4. APOTHEOSIS ELEPHANTINE

Back in the city,
cold noon sun crusting snow,
bladder bursting with fear and fullness,
through the back door of same bright diner,
slouch the hallway to the john.
Inside, the chef stands at the left-most urinal.
He turns, great wanger
three-feet pendulous, half-foot thick.

He plods two-footed out-of-doors,
I follow entranced.
Swooping his cock between the great stumps of his feet,
he writes this message
on the unbroken snow:

> *consider all possibilities,*
> *presume no conclusions.*

Nude Man Tosses Meat from Truck

> Shelbyville, Ind. (UPI)—State
> police arrested a man they said
> stood naked on a moving truck
> in sub-freezing weather and tossed
> sides of beef onto Interstate 74.

Johnson Watson, you sonofabitch,
chucking beef on the highways of America,
blocking the arteries of capitalism—
what were you up to?
Clothed you could have been cagey or malicious,
naked in icy Indiana you had to be mad.

> "Troopers said Watson, 23, hurled
> the meat from an Arora Packing
> Co. refrigeration truck and then
> took off his clothing and threw
> it off, too."

Whatever it was thrown for, or toward,
the meat wasn't enough. Your clothes had to follow
the fat-glistening carcasses.
The wonder is, you didn't throw yourself.

> "When the refrigeration truck
> stopped, the meat thrower jumped
> to the ground and took off."

Johnson Watson, the meat thrower,
terror of the midlands by night:
'Nude man forages smokehouses
of Indiana farms, heaves pork
through kitchen windows . . . .'
'Naked thrower rifles meat cases

→

of Indiana's all-night supermarkets . . . .'

"Trooper Steve Jennings arrested
Watson, who said he was from
Janesville, Wis., and had thrown
· the meat to 'feed the people.'"

Johnson Watson, the Robin Hood of beef!
You envisioned the peasants of America
gathering the venison of the New World,
but they didn't come.
Best thing for you, Johnson.
There would never have been enough.
They would have ripped the meat
and stuffed it in their gas tanks
to fuel the cars to chase you with.
They would have force-fed your clothing
to their children. They would have taken
you, raw, from the truck.

"He was charged with public in-
decency and malicious trespass."

Democracy, the great leveler,
scythe of America's uneven fields—
Lear would have been jailed before the heath had calmed,
Columbus chained the moment he set foot
on this free and private soil.

My Daughter's Night

—for Heather

Bees in the ceiling's corners,
tree-shadows on your fingers and sheet,
you lie awake from evening until dawn.
Your little sister sleeps beside you
while strings of black air push through
the window screen to tangle
with voices from walls
and drop quivering in a dark mass
on the dresser across the room.

Though you are nearly seven, you won't believe
you sleep. How do I explain
what I cannot show you?
Perhaps while my nights are elsewhere
you know the dark as being here.

Your pillow rushes against your ear
like the ocean shell in your closet.
You lie in thought until the daylight
brings us back to you from our waste of sleep.

When you're old, what will matter—
that you were always awake,
or that you could never dream?

Tracking Deer with My Daughters

—for Heather and Miranda

From the porch we watched them bound
across the long yard and full-tilt,
somehow, through these branches
even a six-year-old must lift aside.

I show you the cleft twin-pointed prints
inch-deep in the pine forest loam.
Where the ground goes hard
along a small ridge, mounds of needles
mark the strikes of running hooves.

You track downhill from the house,
refuse to turn back
until a fence and creek arrowhead before us.

A twig snaps in the thicket
beyond the creek. You set your patience
against the deer's—I, mine against yours.
And nothing happens.

And the buzz of insects blends
with that pressure in the forehead
you do not feel—
that humming of moments
when, knowing nothing else, we know
some gain or loss is taking place.

Tomorrow, the apples on the lawn
will once more draw the quarry into view,
and having learned pursuit
you will lead me out again.

from

SYNCHRONIZED SWIMMING

(1984)

Synchronized Swimming

After the day's uncertainties, we shape
patterns we are cheered for but cannot see.
Teammates but working alone, we must trust
music and muscle for cadence and touch
to propel our kaleidoscope of limbs,
the flowers and suns of our oiled bodies.
I scull, float, turn, and roll to the dulled beat
reaching me through water. My eye catches
only ceiling, pool bottom, random breast
or cheek or foot of a girl beside me.
"One body!" coach shouts, again and again.
We must believe ourselves a single form, or fail.

Once, a camera hung like a voyeur
above our opening and closing legs,
but when I saw the film—saw no body
as my own to hold or to fear, no mind
but the sweeping points and circles of flesh—
I cried for happiness in the dark room.

Once, when I left the natatorium
to find myself alone on the steep steps
above the cracked street and scattered lights,
children came to me. They touched me and cheered.
It was as if I could expand for them
there on that grimy stoop, link us all
for some radiant work in the world.

I. *Learning to Live in America*

The Birth of Christ

Beyond the long tables lined with tiny chairs,
the uncurtained stage rises above the lunchroom floor.
Wearing their coats, polite parents sweat through every number.

When two first graders enter alone,
the audience stops its undercurrent mumble.
The girl, head bowed and draped,
watches only the bundle in her arms,
seats herself in the lone chair center-stage.
Joseph follows, shoulders straight, and kneels beside her.

Handel's *Hallelujah* scratches and spreads above us.
Across three hundred years something reaches
to pull us, shuffling but silent, to our feet.

When the music ends we carry our silence
to the cars by the gym's high wall.
Our dozens of white breaths
puff toward the sky in chorus,
and in the darkness glint the stars
we had not noticed when we came.

Chicken in a Florida City

There is a chicken outside
the Krispy Kreme doughnut store.
5:00 a.m. tends to be the same
along the suburban avenues
in this medium-sized city,
but this dawn features a chicken.

He paces the concrete surrounding the store.
The workmen keep quiet
as they get their coffee,
but when the young children
begin to arrive at seven o'clock,
they hop and shout: "There's a chicken out there!
Why is there a chicken out there?"
The Egyptian woman behind the counter
leans to see, but can only shrug.
This is not *her* country.
The parents grimace,
press down on their children's shoulders,
and order the usual.
On the way out no one feeds the chicken.

Flour mills still grind in the Midwest,
cane-presses lift sweet winds over the Caribbean.
No customers plan to change their days.
Tomorrow they will come holding dollar bills
and the curious memory of a chicken.

Learning to Live in America

One seldom thinks of Delaware,
yet surely as the Tetons rise
in any painting, starving dogs
like unicorns roam the streets
of Wilmington, and cabbies joust
on freeways no smaller than our own.
None of us knows anyone
who has walked in North Dakota,
but our glove compartments overflow
with maps we've collected, lined for Bismarck.
We must be ready for Missouri—
the European countries it will hold
in silhouette, the soggy issue of *Time*
in a St. Joseph alleyway,
the girl by the river whose breast glistens
from the touch of her lover's tongue.

The Poetry of American Political Tracts

—for Emily Dickinson and Walt Whitman

> The Japanese used to compose the weightiest
> part of a State document in poetic form.
> —Johan Huizinga

The Articles of Confederation
to be recast in heroic couplets,
the Declaration of Independence
as a Shakespearean sonnet sequence,
the Constitution in loose-lined blank verse
(*We the people of the United States*)
with amendments in westernized haiku.

All subsequent laws and judicial decisions
in freer rhythms—form following function—
until the images of America
crystallize on the bodies of the people
as eagle feathers. Then,
swimming plashless on banks of noon
we look to where our boot-soles left the earth
and hear the prints of brown return to green.

Georgia O'Keeffe's *Blue Morning Glories, New Mexico, II*

Two blossoms, four times natural size.
The one behind opens to the sky, petals
floating like fronds of underwater plants.
Yet for all its large beauty, pale
yellow and white rising into soft, deep blue,
it remains distant, chooses the sun.
The front one blares toward us with its glow—
a gramophone speaker heard through gauze.
In radiant yellow some new language
pours up from the hidden calyx.
No flower has ever been painted before.
If we can wait, we might see Dante emerge
from this shining, his climb to the sky complete.

II. *Fighting Death*

Steam

Never takes the straight path,
but sways and coils in a white dance
to the end of its world.
Waters the garden of your hand
high above the coffee.
Pretends to be smoke
but doesn't suffocate,
Pretends to be winter breath
as it burns your cheek.
Like flames in the fireplace
rises from your cup
to mesmerize, and warm your hands.
Like a love dissolved, never returns
though you stare a hole through the sky.

Listen, My Love

Listen to Edward.
Edward says I write beautiful poems about love.
He is jealous.
He keeps plotting love poems,
but they keep drifting away
to death, politics, trees.
Edward fears his women will leave him,
or never come to him,
because he cannot tell their stories.
He cannot hold them in his poems—
their hands slide off
into political-spectrum symbols,
their bodies become bored as bodies
and turn into rural landscapes.
When I say what my hands feel on you
that they feel nowhere else,
Edward rages with respect.
Every time his hand enters one of his poems,
the flesh drops away.
I comfort him. What he does is good, necessary.
We write of what we fear
or do not understand.

For My First Lover and Her Mother

The traffic light's colors change in the air
above my car stalled near the hospital.
How we are growing undoes what we are—

up in that room with flowers and cancer,
the wall of her mother's room reflects all
the traffic light's colors. Change in the air

is fog beginning, is her daughter's hair
spreading across seven years to recall
how we are. Growing undoes what we are—

you raise your husband's lust someplace out there,
here your mother's cells harvest a ripe hell.
The traffic light's colors change. In the air

the moon shines like your belly's taut skin where
his unborn child presses against my skull—
How we are growing undoes what we are.

You've lain in her stomach and in this car—
all things come down to the strength of a cell.
The traffic light's colors change in the air.
How we are growing undoes what we are.

The Invention of the Villanelle

A tall man lost everything,
started talking to himself.
Found a phrase that comforted,
spoke it now and then for grief.
The words turned against him, pained him.
He found a phrase to fight them with.
Days on end he walked the streets
chanting and taken for mad.
Low-lying clouds pressed down gray,
compacted his grief and speech—
two phrases, four times each,
to save his life. His chanting
taken as music, madness as form.

Nothing But Love Poems Now

You would know why this happens—
why I turn my back to drunks,
refuse to sing with my children,
narrow the world brutally
every time I speak.

For years I believed
in choice, in molding a life
where truth, kindness, and guilt, ignored,
would cut like nails in my shoe.
Now I believe in the rough
swelling disc of your nipple
soft against my obedient tongue,

the words you form to tell me
my life as it's never been,

your eyes' black clamps on my pen.

Deaf and Mute

Safe beyond the edge of the country
we walk the streets and beaches of this island,
off-season guests holding hands fiercely,
inviting the sparse crowd to know that we are lovers.

An old and very local museum
falls victim to our constant laughter
as we tour its chaotic displays:
beneath the photo of a 1920s bowling team,
a glass case with one cow's skull,
one rusted shovel, and one tin bucket.
Handwritten cards beside them read,
respectively, "Old," "Very Old," and "Ancient."
Down the hall, a foot-high copy of the *Pietà*
sits atop a case of military medals;
above the Lord, a photograph of the smiling,
monocled comedian Charles Coburn.

The old deaf curator missed our giggles.
Your breathing and moaning do not pass
beyond this room. On the nightstand
your watchstrap arcs the left lens of my glasses,
both dwarfed by the pink telephone.

And now you sleep curled on your side,
hands tucked beneath your cheek, lips parted.
And I sit watching those lips: everything
they are not saying, all the sense
they cannot make until they touch my skin.
Before today, have we ever heard or said
a single word we could not live without?

Fighting Death

I. *Museum of Her Leaving*

He was collecting things of air—
life preservers, bubbles of soap, balloons—
so their form, emptiness enclosed,
could remind him of her going.

What first demanded search
soon came calling with offerings of air:
His room. His house. Each lawn from there
three hundred miles down the coast.
The world. His lungs. Asking to be filled
with their precious nothing, drained
by cries across the aging table
splintered by scrapings of a thousand cups and plates
in her thousand hands.

II. *Understanding the Future*

The piano begins to play,
discordant before the dawn.
You leave your silent book
to enter the living room
where the cat is in flight
to the floor. You know
she has walked the keys,
yet can prove nothing.
You try to close the piano
but strike the board,
raising the same random sound
that jarred your empty night.
Beyond the fading resound of the room

→

your family sleeps down the long hall,
and you have lost
the one woman
who could carry you through to the end.

III. *Fighting Death*

> "And if I die, who will write
> My poems to you,
> Who will utter the sound
> Of my still-unspoken words?"
> —Anna Akhmatova

1

Once, bullets clicked the leaves above us,
random shots from an unseen hunter.
Our eyes locked as we dressed lying flat.
As we hunched away—I sent you first,
a rare chivalry in my life—
the sounds were so tiny, so clean,
I knew we would be safe.

2

We hated the ocean so always went,
its boring slosh and frightening green
turning us toward ourselves. We walked the beach
as the blind stride the rooms of their own homes,
knowing that nothing will stand in the way.

3

Two others we would call children
walk linked along the street,
her hand curved in his hip pocket,
his elbow resting on her shoulder.
Her long black hair scatters in the wind.
If I call to them, they will hurry off.

4

I sit with words like a kitten
on a floor full of playthings,
leaping from one to another
sparked more by muscle than thought.
Each reach for your love is one
last pull on the slot machine.
Sometime in second grade I learned
I could count till the day I died
and never dent the system.
To speak to you forever,
I would even believe in God.

Divorce

When you die in a northern town
our two graying daughters call me home.
Driving in, I find the strange
countryside and town the same
as places where we met: endless
hills of maple, corn, and cattle,
red-brick streets, high wood-frame houses.
I arrive with my second wife,
my thirty years with her
twice what I had with you.
Only my daughters know me—
our friends different, parents dead,
other relations afraid to come.

Nothing I've known prepared me
for this moment at your grave.
Your second husband four years dead,
I feel, for the first time,
I must be yours again.
Nevermind our thirties,
when youth unraveled
to its opposites—selfishness and fear.
Once, you talked and kissed
only that I might remember, and I do.
By the stone you share with him
my arms encircle our daughters.
Their heads press against my chest
in the vise I have avoided
for so long: difficult love.
The rows of stones radiate from yours.
The sun shone for your burial.
The maples here look healthy,

yet the tips of many branches
hang snapped, as if a storm
had passed through yesterday.

As ever, I don't know how to leave—
which last words to blurt across this mound,
which woman to clutch as I turn,
which wrong choice to make once more.

Belief

—for Roland Flint

> *somehow*
> *in between the wood and wine*
> *there will be no separation,*
> *wood from dark from wine.*

Because my home is long I read your poem
that night as I walked from bedroom to hallway
to foyer. The light in the corridor
faded toward the front of the house.
Your words on the page grew dim,
so when I reached the black doorway
the last word on the page
was the last I could have read—
as if this were the perfect poem,
its wood and wine in step with my life,
its seamless end shivering my skin
because when the doctor said it was a daughter
I was kneeling by my wife's face,
and for a moment, while I had to wait
for his hands to lift from between her legs,
I was father and not-father, with nothing
but belief to tip me either way,
to show me my new life and my old at once,
with nothing but belief joining
the rooms of every home we walk.

The Roland Flint quote is from "Skin" in his collection *Resuming Green: Selected Poems, 1965–1982.*

Counseled by His Readers to Abandon Love Lyrics and Take Up the Real Work of the World in His Writing, He Responds

Say it: a dream saves nothing, walks nowhere—
carries no wood to the thick walls of peace,
to the delicate fires of justice.

Say it: the heart is the greatest trickster,
hawking a lilting form of the world
while small stomachs ache and the dust descends.

Tell me: truth's a bare patch on a distant hill,
a lost spot hidden from my engines of words,
gliding the roads on their honey-slick wheels.

Chide me with visions converted to bone:
Laura, Dark Lady, young Fanny, Maud Gonne.
Quote me the sum of lovers reborn through metaphor.

But listen: if the heart were helium
it would lift me clear of your notions—
sail me, shrinking but shining, toward the evening clouds.

III. *Whatever Light*

Ambition and Hate

—for several friends

You ain't nothing without the right ambition

*****

You ain't nothing without the right hate
(local graffiti)

I. For R. P. D.

Some foreign city glints below—
a fourteen-story drop to the snow
covering the streets and the Boston Commons.
This is April, but no spring blossoms
in memory of salty tea, of Revere,
of a complex dream that started here
and sprawled across the San Andreas Fault.

We have come to this cold history book
for a *convention* of writers, struck
hardly at all but such an irony.
Most of us travel in flocks to parties,
restaurants, lectures, and museums,
pleased by the changes of scene that hum
in all our senses. But you—you hate Boston.

"Everything bad that ever happened
happened here before I was eight."
On Thursday you swear this visit,
your first in twenty years, is the last
for twenty more. By Saturday you've guessed
an old hotel where your father hid away
before he died. You might come back to stay.

→

The uncaught man who murdered your father,
the cancerous lung of your mother
six months later—these were the engines of hate
in a small boy's heart, pistons so great
you could only move on by forgetting
they were always there. But now, their sting
rises through you at fifty-four in this frozen
Boston spring, and what you hate must be chosen,
confronted as the one way forward and back.

I. For G. Z.

> *He has gone where fierce indignation*
> *can lacerate his heart no more*

On our strong and optimistic days
we could believe that such an epitaph
would crown and justify a life,
atone for any sadness that could rise
from our anger at a world whose chaos
not even Swift, so bilious, could devise.

In the lobby of this grand hotel
you find hydrangeas dying in a window box.
Carelessness at the core of opulence
is a fragile, deadly form you know too well:
the choking of the sea, the burning acid of the air,
the radiant refuse in the bomb of the Earth.
As you picket and march and write, your grim faith
is the lioness blocking the mouth of the lair,
standing up to a dozen guns or lances
to gain the last few moments for her young.

You lament hydrangeas in a lonely tongue
whose lexicon is tenderness laced
with anger, the whole speech dropped on a starched cashier
who mouths the world's dreary song—
fault gone elsewhere, well-meaning and empty-faced.
I cannot conceive, much less begin, a comfort to your rage.

III. For D. H.

Keats by his brother's deathbed, breathing
day after day the consumptive air
that would kill him if he left or stayed—
the lush words of a lifetime traded
for the silence of pain, for hair
curled and wet on Tom's pale forehead. Sing
we mustn't, through fear of disturbing
Tom's slow drift into babble—yet sing
we must, for John and his selfless care:
ready to best Milton and Shakespeare,
knowing his greatness was there, a fine thread
he must cut himself like a gray hair
let fall from a window on the evening air.
And no one to touch, or pursue, or hate, but the dead.

Art Elective

—In memory of Miss Proctor

Reflex of memory thrusts
the strong-voweled name *Rouault*
out through my lips as I walk
the hall of my daughter's school
and sight his poster on the wall—
the blocky reds and browns
surrounded by swaths of black,
the squat figures angry
yet somehow sanctified.
I am reminded of style,
how it is rarely taught
but never mistaken once learned,
how I came to it in high school
through luck of scheduling, through Art
Appreciation class—that lone elective
slotted among the requirements.

Old Miss Proctor, green smock
spattered with stringy rainbows,
walked the room like a Pollock miniature.
Her hunched back and wizened face,
the long tables in place of desks,
the full wall of windows—
at first, the class seemed a kindergarten
break, a ball-and-wire cartoon,
Miró amid the testing and the bells.

But Amy was there beside me,
our knees touching beneath the table
we shared in the back-right row.
Our loving scholastic war,
three years old, had never been

so serious and gently fierce
as in those months we learned to sense
the bronze and glow of Rembrandt, to see
the soft-toned lumps of apples and hills—
almost interchangeable, almost alive—
in the many-angled lightings of Cezanne.

The rest of the school was so carefully lit
to protect itself and all of us
from the little darks we were, or might become;
but in Art Appreciation
the dark became the learning space,
holding back the regular light
so the slides could shine and brood
on the luminescent screen above us.
My fingertips were on Amy's thigh,
coming up under her skirt to the edge
where stocking met skin, stunning
border—her hand on me showing
what my hand was doing for her.

Miss Proctor at the bright screen's edge,
pointer and fingers reaching out
to the special blush of blue
that meant Vermeer, "That will mean Vermeer,"
she said, "until the end of the world."
Here, removed from corridors
lined by dull green lockers,
Van Gogh's fiery hills and pinwheels
swirled above the Thirteen Colonies,
the rubbery frogs, the cosines, and the verbs—
and this, we came to know, is style:
the heart of a hand and eye,
knowable though unpredictable,

the shapes and shades we acquire
both with and against our wills.

As if need were impediment to learning
our careful parents lectured us in love—
how it was still a choice for the young,
something not yet hardened by necessity.
But from Blake's acid-etched flames and flowers
arose the palpable words we sought:
You never know what is enough
Unless you know what is more than enough.

While others dawdled and stalled
as if nothing here were tangible,
Amy and I sought perfect scores.
Hour by hour after school
we studied the paintings and sculpture again,
studied the curious notes we'd taken
with our free hands in the dark:
a dozen grids by Mondrian,
his primary colors ruled like cloth
exposed by a microscope;
Gauguin's brown and solid bodies,
ominous and awkward paradise.
And Miss Proctor there at our shoulders,
pressing us even with diction:
"Each piece and detail," she said,
becomes a synecdoche of style."

For just one week she made us
artists, workers in the crafts we observed.
Chalk on heavy paper was my choice,
symbolic abstraction my excuse
for a hand not linked with eye:

a thick, red cross hung high
against blackened air, purple hills
set far below; a jagged graph-line, green,
descending through the cross,
moving left to right into the hills.
The title: "History of Man."
Our final day I abandoned the work,
slashed it with spirals of chalk.
Miss Proctor took it up, championed
its power—swirls and all—to the class.
Amy's thigh gave pressure to mine.
I sat silent, took credit, knowing
Miss Proctor did not believe in accident.
(Her first day's words: *I am an artist.*
My name is Florence.)

I know a man of superb intelligence
who cannot bring himself to eat
a strawberry, although he loves the taste.
As a child he was stricken
by the clear resemblance of strawberries
to his uncle's pocked and bulbous nose;
four decades have not lessened his fear,
his sense of immoral desire . . . .

I watch this poster of Rouault
but see my friend's perverse distress.
I would wish that nose away, would change it
to the breast of my friend's finest lover,
would give him the piling up, the layering,
concocted of dream upon resonant dream—
the writhings of fact made real.

Hearing with My Son

> Our studies show that the autistic child apparently
> has a random relationship with sounds, linking
> them with whatever object holds his attention
> at the moment.

Crouched by his chair, my son hears
my complaint from the wine glass,
my praise from his own shoe.
When I read him books, I speak
through their pictures, or the wall.

Despite my love, I say less and less—
even if he heard me in the trees
or the sunset, he would not listen.

Perhaps, somewhere on the soft and hot
savannahs of Kenya, a newborn gazelle
speaks with the voice of my son.

He throws his cup across the room.
His hand explodes with the crash.

For My Daughters

Inoa Po

One name whispered by the gods
past the hill of the rounded belly:
the given, perfect sound for the child
to carry as comfort and yearning,
the homing pigeon's single place
in the chaos of air and earth.

Come sit on my lap, Miranda.
Miranda, where have you been?
Miranda . . . Miranda.
Be home before dark, Miranda.

If the name we give is wrong
the curses will descend,
and the child cannot answer
wherever the gods may call.
So many other ways to fail,
no excuse to let down on this—
give ear to the hillside, ear to the wind,
to the name of the name for now.

Learning to Make Maps

—for Miranda at 7

Line for the driveway,
box for the church,
bigger box the parking lot,
squiggles for the carport pick-up zone:

your freehand map to lead me
later through the dark
to a place not mine but yours,
shared with a neighbor's child,
regimen of Wednesday nights.

If you've drawn others
I cannot remember when.
This is your mind moving
through the world at last,
going to its places,
bringing its places home.

I remember, from the back seat,
watching my father navigate
the red-brick city streets
and empty country roads
as if he'd never lose the way . . . .

Go on now, in the neighbor's car,
to whatever rites present themselves
to your small and lovely face.
I will be there when you finish.
I promise this map will do.

Music for My Daughters

Beyond all our bounds of monotony
the child lies down each night
to the same record on the tiny machine,
her drowsing and dreams evolving
week after week from identical songs.

She neither thinks of how she chose this theme
nor perceives she will sometime choose another,
but knows she cannot sleep with silence.
When the time comes suddenly for change
she leaves the old music without regret,
with scarcely a thought of the shift—
since the heart of her comfort, the voice
lifted far past speech, remains.

Understanding *King Lear*

When you stir
the blueberry yogurt—

spoon down through
the white cultured yogurt
to the syrup and fruit
underneath,

dark blue-purple rising
first in bursts of color,
then swirling as you stir
into designs of thin-lined
purple and white,
distinction fading
to a deep magenta cream
lumped with blue,
magenta-covered berries—

imagine
Shakespeare's life,
the daily incidents,
the human brilliance.

Freshman Lit & Comp

—for Janet Burroway

Wednesday evenings rooted to his place
—back row, nearest the door—
he had that plodding obstinance
of dullness laced with purpose.
Past twenty-five, pimpled and flabby,
bursting out of himself
at every tuck and button.
Arriving and leaving alone.

Never an answer, never a question,
hauling himself toward me every week
from the wood lathe of his job
in a low-grade furniture shop,
ready for commas, Milton, paragraphs, Donne.
Every other week, another essay
into listlessness and error,
as if the writing meant no more
than the grease he carried on his cuffs.

The *Iliad* provided the finish.
Six years later, I can still paint
the slants and tones of sunlight
mapped across my desk, or sing
the fossils deep below me,
in those moments when I read
his final thesis of our course:

That the truest choice by Homer
was the crippling of Hephaestus,
for only the damaged could understand
the shield scrolled with a gentle iron lace,
the aura that holds around the perfect forging.

A Lecture on E. A. Robinson's "Richard Cory"

The brilliance of complete things
we often find resides, actually,
in a single piece of the whole.
As in "Richard Cory," where the horrible
power is in the simple word *put*:

> *And Richard Cory, one calm summer night,*
> *went home and put a bullet through his head.*

Not *blasted*, not *fired*, not even *drove*.
We can envision a man
holding a bullet between fingers and thumb,
and pushing it into his brain.
The splitting of the skull, the gush of blood,
the slow grinding through bone
until the slug pops easily
into the soft cortex.
This is a man *putting* a bullet—
a man getting through another moment
of his life, one which is coincidentally,
as it turns out, the last he will ever know.

Gladys

Something in her sharp face made me nervous.
I was seventeen—my first time-card work—
and each morning when I punched in Gladys
was there on her stool near the loading dock.
She was a sander, handling tiny parts
die-cast at the rear of the plant: levers
for voting machines, hasps of twenty sorts.
Working piece-rate, her fingers were fliers
near my gimp thumbs on the huge press machine.
I trimmed waste like an axe-man dropping heads,
she soothed and buffed steel with a touch so fine
you'd wish her always in your midnight bed.
But her face—the first I'd seen with youth so thin
I stared each morning to see if it was gone.

Bread

—for Susan

There will be bread no matter what,
so you choose to mourn with flour
powdering your hairline,
with your hands shredded by strings of dough.
You can dream the desert of Moses,
the beehive ovens of Africa,
the softest croissants of erotic days—
anything but this chilling house,
the death of your closest friend.
You mourn through the beat of your hands' kneading,
for the unbroken history of bread
is neither accident nor wonder,
but the survival of simplicity:
bread was our purest creation,
flour transformed by water and fire.

Someone watching from across the yard ·
or high above the reddening autumn trees
could not know what special grain you breed—
the sour tang of rye, the sweet heaviness of white—
but would know each grows from grief,
that single soil we always walk.

As the smooth loaves warm and swell
under the dampened cloth, and the oven's heat
drifts to adjoining rooms, you give yourself
a moment to believe in miracles.
But your aching hands recall you
to the work this day has been,
while the dried and cracking film of dough
stiffens your fingers until they seem,

themselves, the residue of failure.
In the burning water from the faucet
you scrub your skin and scrape your nails
as if somehow they could come to match
the rising gold of the oven's loaf.

But the full beauty of bread
resides in its consumption,
and you know the threat of weeks to come:
you will raise a hand to point directions,
or you will circle your lover's neck
until your hand comes close to your face,
and there, buried beneath the nail
like a shard of your own bones,
the last dried speck of dough—
the savior that cracks your heart.

Spreading My Father's Ashes

ASGARD—VALHALLA,

PRIVATE DRIVEWAY

We touch again—
my hand dips and clutches,
fist full
yet fingers nearly down flat
against the palm.
Hand raised, fingers sprung.

You phony bastard,
why didn't you tell them
about this place—
tell them how you loved it?
Big-shit Swede,
off the boat and into the money:
"Know more about their money than they do,
they'll have to share it with you."
Philosopher, disguised as phony bastard
Certified Public Accountant.

Dropping becomes throwing
as the path circles back to the cabin,
the circuit of the land
more finished than the task.
I aim for things, but miss.
A wind-shift fires one throwing
straight back in my face.

Crazy son-of-a-bitch,
head of the firm,
long workdays torn by debit and credit,
raging existentialism once each year
at your office Christmas party

on a quart of Scotch,
preaching to dazed CPAs
the death of God, the joke of Christ—
then driving drunk to this place,
sleeping it all off,
waking to a snowy day of great peace.

Last shaking and whacking,
the upside-down urn;
hands rinsed by icy pump-water,
dried with broad rubbings across old jeans.
My hands are clean.

I watch the damp on my thighs,
the water-darkened cloth
streaked white by faint remnants of ash.

Water-Shadow

We know not why or what, yet weave, forever weave.
—Walt Whitman

On a sunny day it would be shadow,
this needle-fine web of moisture
near the pavement's edge
beneath the evergreens.
But dew and later clouds
made the pines protect the road today
not from glare but from drying,
leaving this lace of water
as a fossil of the night.

Though asphalt and earth ask nothing,
I could bare my chest and lay it
against this odd morning map.
The deep weave of my veins
would match the Earth as if mirrored—
a moment of dreams and regrets,
the thoughts of a Siamese twin
as the surgeon's knife comes down.

Epitaphs

In memory of John Hamilton Reynolds
(1794-1852), who chose to be identified on
his tombstone only as The Friend of Keats.

We all have this final chance to speak:
Here, under the wide oaks preserved
as if shade and coolness were honor
for the dead. Or here, in this flat space
burning beneath the sun, open
to that sun as only broad water
should be open. Or here, crowded
upon a tilted, corroding stone
in sight of the country church.

Books and letters can serve, shelved
apart from acid and ice and rain,
but only our last stone words can rest
within sounding distance of our bones.
We need science but no religion to know
how the timbre and pitch of any voice,
reciting our words with face bent downward,
will pass waves through the ground—
will resonate against us
in the pattern of our chosen sounds.
Yet we opt for the relative silence
put forth by a name and two dates,
or we settle for standardized blessings:

God-fearing Man

*

Dear, Loving Mother

*

Resting This Hour with God

John Hamilton Reynolds, I say
there are better voices than these—
better for the human, for any divines.

Something from our own repeated speech:

> *18 seasons*
> *with the pharmacy softball team,*
> *13 and 12 in our only winning year.*

*

> *Janice, where in the hell*
> *are my goddamned shoes?*

Something from what we had meant to say:

> *Whenever you were not looking,*
> *for all those years,*
> *I studied the ways of light*
> *against your hair.*

Or something we would never speak
in any other place or way:

> *For all I knew and tried,*
> *I never learned to distinguish*
> *silence from truth,*
> *speech from the urge to speak.*

Yet for you, Reynolds, *The Friend of Keats*,
not even these would have been enough.

Walk away to the world,
you seem to have said.
Set another, always, before you.

The sun and the mirror serve,
but must not be stared at.

How Poets Would Have Us Know Them

As we read calligraphy,
where pressure, angle, and nib
free beauty from sense.

As we shiver
to the voice of a certain singer,
always wanting more,
nevermind the words.

As we rise
to a lover's hand as it nears,
though we do not know
what the stroke this time will be—
though the lover may be gone,
the hand in our dreams alone.

from

All These Lands You Call One Country

(1992)

I. *Attacking the* Pietà

Failure to Be Priests: A Modern Harvest

. . . as a stallion stalwart, very-violet-sweet
—Gerard Manley Hopkins

If we do not see the horses fraught with flowers,
the musical fire of invisible hummingbirds,
the graceful, loping gait of tombstones crossing fields,
it is from our stagnant fear of mockery—
our worry to be right, and righteous, and exact—
our failure, once again, to be priests.

We know this globe that could be a mushroom
might not be at all—sprouting fast but scarcely quick
into the far blue air we have come to call God's face—
so now we find that all we can believe
is so much less than all, is shadowed and shackled
by dark and thinning thought, by chains of flimsy logic
closing off the organ's pipes to still
our outrageous music, our glorious tin-turned-to-golden singing.

Past, Present, Future

Like the burn of sex we want it again—
that moment from the past we thought we had
but lost, jolted, as we lose at waking

the wisp that led to nightmare's tears or screaming.
That day, or hour, seemed a rock in the hand.
Like the burn of sex, we want it again

and again, our whole lives' narrow-track bodies
never bored by lust, by memories' clutch—
those sun-hot monuments to *have* turned *had*.

Miles-long view from hill, taste of milk or rain,
wind-cut face, parents alive without pain—
these we covet, like the burn of sex, again . . . .

Dear Reader, this is not what you think,
not bedroom talk nor family-album time
flipping through stacked moments we'd wish ahead.

No, this is the passing world, which had a history
until we turned against the future,
bludgeoned both—*was* and *might be*—with the present:
Stunned moments and thoughts. Burned-out sex. Had. Have not.
    Won't.

Attacking the *Pietà*

On May 21, 1972, Michelangelo's Vatican *Pietà* was assaulted
by Lazlo Toth, 33, a Hungarian-born geologist who scaled
a marble balustrade in St. Peter's Basilica and lashed out
with a hammer, crying "I am Jesus Christ!"

1.   Michelangelo Begins

His first blow to the block shows nothing
yet still is a start toward shape—
thought to thing, edge to curve,
world from the hard, blank earth.
The one piece of his life
on which he will carve his name.
Spurred by his fear of the graven image,
of the easy ways the righteous go astray
when thought and act diverge,
he guides his perfect slab into perfection.

2.   New York World's Fair, 1964

When I was sixteen, I gave in
to my parents' hands steering my shoulders
away from the food and the hoopla of nations,
let myself be led to the still lines
waiting in the August heat.
I felt the cold presence of the building
as we entered and stepped on the moving belt.

Floating slowly on our dark way,
I thought how the statue was always noise
until the chisel's final glancing,
how quiet suddenly filled his room
with completion designed to last
in a world I could not imagine.

→

But Michelangelo Buonarroti, knowing
things are always waiting to emerge,
might well understand the conveyor
sliding us from sunlight to sunlight
in seven minutes of night—a chip of silence
gathered from Gotham's astounding mass.
He might accept the great glass wall
rising to hold back everything,
including the bullets he had never seen.
He might even sense this belt and window
to have grown from the statue itself:
the swell of completion and isolation
loosed by his own hands,
the *noli me tangere* feeding our awe.

3.   The Schooling of Lazlo Toth

Layers were always his life.
His mother buried him with blankets
so that dark became heat and weight,
then sang and peeled them one by one,
calling him back to her fact and light—
his small back arching from the bed
in a child's hope of levitation,
knowing how in seconds he'd be free.

For Hungarian winter she wrapped him:
stockings and socks and woolens,
shirts and sweaters and coats.
Out through the icy streets and back,
gently stripped at her hands before the fire—
his body emerging from its mummied stance,

warmer and warmer the less it wore.
On one walk he fell and was bruised
even through the clothing's cushion.
The rock-point's damage hurt him more
with every garment she lifted off,
as if the wound were really growing
from her hands. But when it lay revealed,
a dull red shine like the stove's,
her hands were the only comfort.

The great gash of cliff above their town:
picnics at its base, climbs to the top
through the grassy slopes behind the face.
His father always pointing out the crush
laid by time on rock, the dull and shimmering veins;
his notion born for giving life to stone
by learning to speak its names and depths.
Tied by ropes to the roots above,
they'd edge down fissures
until from the top they looked,
Mother said, like heads rolling on the grass.
Then farther down, Father saying stretch
your fingers wide and lay them flat
and touch more years than Man has walked the Earth.

4.   Nineteenth Century: The Priests Improve the Statue

If the shepherds stray, shall the sheep be blamed
for straying likewise?

Hail Mary, full of grace and brackets . . . .

→

In the hearts of the holy fathers
the need for haloes was discerned
and the means discovered: Christ the tricky
job with his head supine, drilled
through the top and plugged with a rod,
the shining metal circle affixed.
Mary with clamps at her nape—
the cliffs of Carrara moaning in the wind,
the haloes pulsing sickly light
for the eyes of the blind.

5.   The Song of Lazlo Toth

It was Her. Him I would not touch,
the One who suffered, who was dead and sagged
on that hand that had never not touched Him.
But Her. That face so at ease, so glib,
bowed as if thinking of a story
She's heard, and trying to be sad.
Never hungry in Her life, never alone.
I went for the eyes—you've seen them?
Up close? Beneath those lids—nothing!

The stone cried for release, and I came.
The papers say fifteen times, or eleven.
It was again and again, and never enough.
Her arm hitting the floor was beauty itself.

My mother starved while guards were paid
to strut St. Peter's for the sake of rock.
Buonarroti, your hands are dust.
If I had found that slab on the beach,

oddly shaped by the tumblings of God,
I'd have heaved it straight back to the sea.

6.   Photographer

She was a new shot each time that he swung:
small pocks like craters opening,
one by one, in the softness of stone;
her arm at the instant it fell.
I never thought to look away
or run him down, took my eye
from the zoom lens only once—
discovered then the scene's failure,
the loss of tight detail.

Soon she would be coddled, remade
in her own image, glorious
fake that her maker alone might detect.
Only at first was she mine: my shutters
opened her far beyond
any vision that Joseph had known.

7.   Souvenir Hunter's Prayer

The hole in my hand
throbs and exists
in my thoughts alone—
those fearing storms
need no storms to fear.
I know what I have—
body of God's mother—
and where it belongs.

→

I watched them all on their knees
on ladders the following day:
picking through the piled-up wax
crusting the holders and walls,
dreamers on a fantastic dig.

Define a true relic?
One that cannot be held.
Returning to the Dome,
approaching the curate,
I'll grope for the right word:
Shard. Fragment. Chip. Fleck.
Let him deal with it—
glue it back, toss it away.
At least I know my meanings
when they have burned me.
May all others learn
this much. Amen.

8.   The Restorers' Debate

i

Truest creation obliges us all
to enter the world it has made. Come hell
or high water, heaven or searing drought,
we must acknowledge the power of heart
crossed with starred hands and gifted intellect:
such sacred projects are forever flecked
golden by special light, never to be
destroyed or stolen, never to be
equaled in their spirits or their honed skills.
But what they are, they *must* remain through time:

we have the means to save appearances,
must dutifully reclaim originals
from accidents, war, and weather—from slime
walking in human form, doing the devil's dance.

ii

Just to feel her this way is far too much,
running my fingers over the hard stump
left below her shoulder, forcing my touch
on the shattered nose's triangular hump—
all this in the name of gaining some sense
for matching up these grainy surfaces
with the chunks and splinters I'll dandle next,
as if such art could be jigsaw pieces.
To repair her would imply that she *works*
like some engine or ceramic jug,
and that she was merely *made* for our gawks,
anonymous plaster donkey or dog.
The artist's sacred circle shelters all—
creates the rise, encompasses the fall.

9.   Lurleen Wallace Considers the News
      at Her Sleeping Husband's Bedside

So here is what another six days can make:
George with a promise of life, though frozen forever—
that bastard Bremer's bullet a nail
driving our spines to a clicking and humming chair.
And now this statue, shattered and cried for everywhere,
shrouded and placed in the hands of restorers

→

whose money and months will give her perfection again.
Arthur Bremer. Lazlo Toth. How many names for hate!

George, this commentator speaks of art and life,
says that many will weep for rock yet not for you,
says there are things that cannot be replaced
and things that cannot be replaced.
George, I wish I didn't want to read this,
wish I didn't have these photos of the whole and broken.
He says, "Forgive me, please, but money makes the world—
her art, her politics and sex—go 'round."
He says the Vatican invested wealth in art
believing in a visual ride to heaven,
says we tried the identical trip
on the sweating backs of slaves.
Says every assassin has been poor, or afraid of poverty.

Christ, George, what does anyone know
unless he's lived at the center and on top at once?
Remember how you told me we could rise and rise,
carrying the righteous with us
while the empty fell away below?
I swear I don't know anything, except
the world is what those who make it make it.
Yes, I'll run for governor—
me your back and you my tongue,
holding each other up as we must.

10.   *Pietà*: For My Father

This will not be easy, this denouncing.

So much of what he felt was always right
in that second, midnight world
where accountant would be architect—
the ciphers and terms of analysis raised
to envisioning forms in space,
to clothing the air itself.

*

Sketching on the backs of his ledger sheets
the vaultings of buildings or a vibrating pillow
to waken the hard of hearing,
my father had dreams of invention and craft.
Just married, he stood at the white mountain
raised by a snow-covered stockpile of coal,
and there—as my mother sat miles away,
darning socks while chicken baked in the cramped kitchen—
he learned the bounds of imagination
for junior accountants on inventory jobs:
pacing off and sighting up the hill,
poking the depths of snow with sticks,
concocting his own equations and stats,
he managed a figure too clear and close
for the day's adverse conditions;
juggling his own numbers to back off from truth,
he was hailed for exacting work.

*

In the shadowed light of that moon called *blue*
we may rise to occasional wisdom.
That morning in 1972,
above the rounds of muffins and eggs.
I raised my section of the paper to counter his.
lWe had always been a cartoon breakfast—
my father an expanse of newsprint
fringed by sets of fingers and wreathed by smoke,
Mother the quiet shuffler, cooking and pouring.
Growing up, I had envied the great
Italian families in movies, yakking and laughing
across a long, massive table,
inventing their days at breakfast
and recounting them there at night.
But silence was our usual word,
even in those later years
when I came to table as visitor,
sprawling my legs in the space beneath—
the open shell of a family grown.

That one day in 1972,
the rare cry of print
only the avid can hear as they read:
the Blessed Virgin pummeled and split—
not in her spirit, for which I had no use,
but in her body of art, irreplaceable.
Across the table, I counted
on my father's second self to rise to my call,
but he shrugged aside my sorrow
at the fury of Lazlo Toth,
turned again to the things of his world.

*

My loss was not the indifference
but the fragile void of its causes,
the way a life we love can be steered,
beyond our control, beyond us.

I thought how stately and sprawling old homes in the country,
accosted now by highways jammed up to their porches,
surely must be among the saddest things on Earth.
They are what they were yet are utterly changed,
webbed in the world that made them,
nothing but all they have to be.

If one needs all his life
to write each poem, this only says
his entire life is what he needs
for anything he'll ever do.
We wear the past like leaded boots
on astronauts who walk the moon—
the heavy exertion of every step
our only chance to keep from drifting off.

II. from *Li Po and Tu Fu in America*

Li Po and Tu Fu Arrive by Jet over California

Leavings mold the deepest songs.
Countless roads here stretch away
To places we've not yet left.
This may be a good country.

Famous Mountains

> I would tend a white deer on the green cliff
> And ride it whenever I visit famous mountains.

1. Mount Rushmore

Faces flower on the cliff.
Swarming people here below
Tell me these buds are sculptures
They've crossed the country to see.
Do horses race into fire?
Will men abandon their homes
To stand and stare at rock?
No, my friends . . . these are blossoms
In an orchard of your dreams
You would set flight toward forever.

2. Tu Fu at Pike's Peak

> *An imperishable fame of a thousand years*
> *Is but a paltry, after-life affair.*

Who could ever guess
What a man must do
To become a mountain?

I stare from a distance
Toward the solitary peak,
Chanting the beautiful word,
Zebulon, Zebulon.

Small children in bright shirts
Scramble on the lowest slopes,

Top a ledge, and raise their arms.
As if it were the summit.

In Szechwan a man spent his life
Discovering streams in hidden places,
Giving every one his name.

Zebulon, Zebulon—
When you journeyed homeward,
How much of you returned?
What lay by your wife in the night?

Cars and trailers grind your skin,
Oil seeps toward your great heart,
Your sweet first name is forgotten.

Did you turn even once from your wife,
From her touch or your children's eyes,
To the mountain you had claimed
Like a fool who gathers shiny stones,
Then tries to spend them in the marketplace?

In Szechwan the stream-finder died,
An old man beside quick water
That bore his name into the distance.
He did not know which stream that was.
They never found him—never.

3. In the Great Smoky Mountains

Rocks as large as temples
Fill the streams swirling down

Through silence and rhododendron.
We walk three hours and see no man.

Five miles away
Tourists pack the streets,
Ceramic faces of Christ
Filling the windows of Gatlinburg.

These are your country's spaces,
Almost larger than the world itself.
Is it not a man's nightmare
To enter a room in his home
And find it completely strange,
As if he'd wakened in the night
To his wife as a stony grave?

Learning

More sighing for the clumsiness of my life's course

Friends have walked the high cliff's edge,
Their outlines against the sky or moon
As they flowed so slowly away, leaving me
Weeping beside others who might soon depart.
One thing I was taught as a child:
"Life is learning to let things go."
And I find I am always learning.
Your gray poet—the newer, not the first—
Wrote, "Nothing gold can stay."
I will carry home these words,
Speak them when I see and embrace
Those friends I left behind in tears.
I will tell them how I stood
On your Great Divide and felt
At home in a way I'd never known:
After all the years of one foot, other foot,
One foot—that awkward and rolling
Forward dance of travel—I thought
I had found a place of balance,
A home for this ungainly stride
I've been given, and must call my life.

Travels in Two Worlds

Secluded things are, after all, a joy.

Your great cities seem to echo
Through the furthest canyons and plains,
So our riding across the desert comes to be
Not rest from the clutter of overrun streets,
But a pause between them. We seldom look
To the air around us, but watch the horizon
Ahead for the haze of our destination.

In the garden of my birthplace long ago,
I never thought of how we had so many trees,
for anytime I was there I was leaning against just one.
When my mother entered through the gate,
She was the only person in the world.

Loneliness and forgetting are called for
In your country, but hard to find and keep
Because they are sought so consciously.
I have taken well to your language,
Yet among that store of words
I have not fathomed these:
Vacation. Getaway. Break.

Li Po Enters New York City

I have been accepting all
These lands you call one country.
Sometimes I have had to say *dream*,
Softly to myself, even when sober;
Yet I have gotten along
Watching the faces and horizons,
Touching coarse leaves and barks,
Lifting curious objects from countless shelves.

But this, the sky-reaching beast
At the end of the river-pressed tunnel,
Is more dream than anyone can stand.
(What if every man who passed
Would offer me some wine?
What if great rivers ran
In some land atop these buildings,
Then roared down here and there
As the world's most delicate falls?)
Carriages roll crisply along
Amongst the mad crush of autos,
Skeletons stumble dazed on the sidewalks
Alongside the arrogant wealthy;
Everywhere things and things and things—
Traded for paper peeled like membrane
From the heart, for coins shaken
Like polished bones in a dicing cup.

I am told there was a man
In yet another country
Who spoke for me, one Socrates.
Passing through the Athenian market
He paused to take in every sight,
Then turned to his shadowing disciples:
I never knew there could be so many things
I did not want.

Changes

> How like a bolt of white silk is this water,
> Turning the earth into a flattened sky.

These north Maine woods are dressed
Like certain provinces at home:
The craggy pines, the steep rocky cuts
Down to fast water, the sun cool
Even at his highest arcing.
Still, miles away is nothing we ever see—
The frightening coasts of boulder and spray.
I go there to drive out longing,
To be alone in the strangeness.
And yet, some days I see the fishermen
Near and far offshore, and home grips me
Once again, needing only the smallest cause.
So many times I have commanded the Earth,
"Stay what you are! Become nothing else!"
But always there is changing: old into new
And new into old, water to silk
Worn by the cloud-strewn earth.

Prayer for Offering Prayer

> Blue is the smoke of war, white the bones of men.

For this one gift alone—
No living memory of war
Touching your endless soil—
You should be a country of priests.
No fields burned by the angry
Enemy torch, its holder dreaming
His own far-off hills
Might be suffering the same this moment.
No staved-in doors, no sleep lost
Over a night-time invasion
Shattering cups in your own kitchen.
No children walking the dirt streets,
Dazed, skirts in tatters past their knees.

I have learned your history,
Know the old tinge and twinge
You carry, the wars for selfhood
And the war of self divided.
I have learned music from the South
Proclaiming that war still thrives,
But I mount my donkey and ride
Away, laughing quietly at fools.
I scan the sky for blue on blue—
Smoke on the autumn clarity—
But there is only one shade.
My donkey steps gingerly,
But never to avoid strewn carcasses.
Bones are deep now, buried
As few nations can imagine.

Shameless America

Lost among flowers, I wear a hat upside-down.

It would seem that nothing shames you,
And I thought at first this was good.
You have still the great spaces
For movement and escape, for running
Naked or foolishly clothed.
Out from the black streets to the brown,
Out from the concrete toward rock,
You dare to turn from anything
You have done or allowed to happen.
To start, I was with you at every step,
Wine jug in my hand as we wound
Together through fields and among sparse trees.
You felt no sadness or hesitation
For the dark things you had achieved,
So you wore your shirt buttoned behind.
I set my cap upon its closed side
And pressed it down over my skull,
Thinking at first to play, but knowing soon
I was really praying for us all:
This too-large country with its strangers
Falsely linked by wires and pictures.
These hidden hates. This very air
Filled and smudged with guilt.

Exile

An owl calls from a brown mulberry,
Field mice fold their paws in a mess of nests.

Everywhere I turn I find homes:
Nests and burrows, sheltered corners,
Pockholes in sand, knotholes in bark.
I walk onward, only to find more homes—
Beaver cave tucked beneath its crowned dam,
Bear cave creviced on the hillside.
Beyond the path-filled, nest-filled forest.
I'll come to the closed-in city:
Sheds and shanties, mansions
In their own forests, stacks of dwellings
Rising toward the cloud-roofed sky.
I walk farther on, and farther still.
I came here to learn,
But there are days when learning means nothing.

The Last Journey

Ready to return home, he could not bear to leave;
Tears flow as he bids farewell to herons and ducks.

As a young man I was driven
From my home, sent across river and mountain
Away from all friends and trees.
I carried my wineskin plus clothes for a week,
Knowing I could never carry enough.
I embraced my friends and was gone.
I hated new trees for the love of old,
Tucked my arms to my sides
Lamenting the ways they had clutched before.
But soon there was spring, and then summer,
In all the next valleys I reached.
Loving still my old Szechwan,
I saw I could love each place I stood,
Each person I met or passed,
With baffled, baffling energy.

III. *The Blooming of Sentimentality*

Ars Poetica

Once I let something die.
It stank so, and so
pervasively, it entered
even my closets and dreams.

Then I vowed to keep all things
breathing and moving, hook
my arms beneath their shoulders,
walk and walk and walk them down
the rinsed and shining corridors.

The Blooming of Sentimentality

I hear it coming from the start,
the claptrap all shamelessly marshalled:
the hordes of muted violins
swelling and subsiding, the voice
wrenching to a wail I know
makes a cheap-shot bid for my heart.

I keep it all at a distance,
looking askance at the hangdog eyes
or the child's squeal and her sparkling smile—
these images that must not count
because they are designed to count,
to demand the shiver of my skin
for the whimper of a half-pound pup.

Time after time I fend it off,
the chorus of grandmothers, roses, and tears.
It seems to fall from the sky,
to sprout from the ground by night—
rootless, and puffed with hope.
I focus instead on integrity:
wholeness and balance of mood,
visions that come from those depths
where freshness and honesty breed,
where clans of thin motives and still-thinner words
lack the power and desire to go.

But on one dark, soulful day
those violins rise up again,
so many that I picture a wave,
the sweeping bows like grain
rippling to the far horizon.
And through that deafening swell,
my lovers and family march uphill

to a flowered ridge glued on a crystal sky,
where the Enemies cannot reach them.
This *could* be the place, I suddenly think,
and I run to reach that distant height,
my arms outstretched and raised
in that gesture of exaltation
I have always seen but never known.
And then, I am beside myself as well,
cheering me on as I run.

I reach the sun-drenched edge and I know
I have cut off the dullness of reason
to set loose a burgeoning dream
that could give all my other dreams range.

Sampler of a Father's Wisdom

Dale Burton Corey, 1925-1985

You must allow only the still
photographs. For all the family, for good
friends whenever possible,
shun the moving pictures—
hauntings unbearable
with their swooping arms, flipping
leaves, open and shaping lips
when I am flat stone gone.
                    *

Though I might say otherwise,
there are no foolish fears.
Even in our own backyard, the darkness holds
whatever you hear or feel, whatever
the words of others cannot dispel.
Ignore my coldness and seeming anger
at your cringings from bushes and trees;
I will soon think twice, will hold you
close for all we cannot hold at bay.
                    *

Double-knot the basic shoestring bow
before each run or game.
You give up ease of loosening,
a certain floppy grace
to the loops and strands
as they toss and wilt with your moves.
You gain a shoe that's constant—
banking firmly through corner twists,
tearing mud from the Earth—
a shoe that grips till dark on summer's longest day.

                    *

No white clothing—ever.
The dirt grinds in,
shadows the fabric with dinge
communion girls have cried for,
having no choice at the final hour
but to quiver down the aisles
as if the white were white.

*

Whenever live wires are involved
overlap your windings by half
or more, pulling the black tape taut.
For safety turn and turn
until your fingers ache.
The greater the force, the deeper
it must be buried. Power you need,
but arm and build to hold down shock.

*

Driving on any ice, abandon
whatever logic you know:
Turn toward the fishtail
to straighten, stay off the brake
when you're losing all control.

*

In pursuing grief, a slow gathering
is the only way, as if we'd find it
in the form of the three-toed sloth:
barely seeming to move from hour to hour,
yet earning a place in all our books
when we picture the strange and unique.

Not for Clennie (1901–   )

Our birth is but a sleep and forgetting . . .

As we photograph an infant
(startled by the pointless flash)
only for ourselves, so this is not for you
newly set in this nursing home,
your entire life squeezed
out and away by sclerotic growth.

Through recent months you got along with lists
naming your son and daughter as son, daughter;
naming their children, your parents,
others from your own far past
we ourselves could not recall unaided.
Of late, the alphabet is drained
of all, for you, but shapes and blackness—
our names and faces reborn to your eye
with perfect and grim democracy.

My wife once nursed a woman caught
by the rare trap of scleroderma, wrapped
in her own skin's unthinkable hardening—
Pygmalion's nightmare alive.

Clennie, if still you were wholly here
what equation might you make
to weigh such losses,
body versus mind?
I speak and am nothing
to your failing ears among the many voices,
am loudness and pitch alone.
My only choices, my only chances
in the end:

To strike no tone
 that gives you cause to worry,
to be quiet
wind or music at your ear.

Town and Country Losses

He had been only John,
pumping gas at the Keystone
near my parents' home.
Probably two years older than I,
and just out of school.
Nozzle in and on.
Me standing by waiting,
cocky and impatient to be moving,
new license burning my pocket
like the hand of God or my girl.
Nozzle off and out.
                          And then—
after six months of not knowing
I hadn't seen him lately—
I found his face curled up on my lawn
when I picked up the morning paper.
Front-page news: "Local Serviceman
Killed on Vietnam's Hamburger Hill."
His company at the lead edge,
storming to take the strategic mound
in a single afternoon.
Next day, the dead and the living
descended together—
the hill not needed
after all.

I walked back toward the house
thinking how late it was
in this factory town—6:30—
to hear no cars going by.
Thinking of the last time I'd cried,
five years before at my grandfather's death—
not at the funeral,
but in front of the television

when my parents brought the news,
where I'd been earlier trying
to talk to God about what
I would do if only this one time . . .
thinking of all those years I'd spent
at bowling alleys and softball fields,
wishing for shirts with my own first name
blazoned above the pocket.

As a paperboy I'd folded and tucked
eighty copies in the pre-dawn dark,
creased the same stories
over and over, thrown them at all
those quiet, undisturbed doors.
My arm cocking and aiming and releasing:
strange marches in the faraway South,
Wilt Chamberlain's 100-point game,
my own brother's birth.

Back inside, the way
to the kitchen table was too long,
the cornflakes box too tall.
My mother jerked across the room,
housecoat too yellow.
I held my breath a few seconds,
then a little longer each time.
Reaching for the milk I hit
the tomato juice pitcher,
sending shattered glass and redness
everywhere. And then I was shouting—
screaming—word after word
mother had never heard from me once,

let alone over and over.
She kept trying to quiet me.
"It's nothing," she said.
"Don't worry, it's all right.
There's more, there's plenty more."

I Find That Mother Begins

—for Julienne Barbara Corey, 1926-2003

Have you considered lately our various jokes
on the sleeping, the ways we sometimes gather near
their otherness, their intimate removal, to watch or mimic?

I'm thinking not only of drunks in the park—
gaunt and greasy magnets holding a splay of children
drawn from the swings and ballfields to dance
with wildest gestures of face and arm—
I'm looking also into living rooms, to the quiet creeping
the young ones will make toward their father
as he readies for evening with a dinnertime nap,
their silent, giggling conspiracy bent
on repeating his every twitching and snort and flop.

And then I am thinking of all
the familiar travelers, wounded birds
who let us come near in unthinkable ways:

>   The strangers on buses and trains, their heads rolling
>   through tense, jerky circles we ogle with stories
>   that guess how their lives might have gotten them here.

>   The newborns whose days are nearly defined as sleep,
>   giving us time, as we stare, to adjust to their presence.

>   A sleeping lover as we watch in the early light—
>   making, in stillness and silence, our offerings
>   once again of every pleasure and hope.

I know there is a part we were not told
in the story of the Sleeping Beauty:

how the Prince camped out for days that rolled into weeks
at the glass-walled tomb, leaning this way and that
as he stared, trying to make the choice
between riding off and reaching out—perfection and possession.

In the room beyond where I sit this this early morning, Mother begins
a raucous and ugly snoring, sounds she's never made
but had slept beside for forty years. Now, his heart having failed
in the winter past on Inauguration Day,
she begins to wake him as she can:

Turning over into the space of his absence,
though turning in a way and time she does not know.
Making his body's dumb music her own.

For the Spreading Laurel Tree

—to my daughter Heather

> "Here is the hurt
> and how it lasts forever."
> —Lee K. Abbott

Math be damned, numbers are never equal:
two years gouged from fifteen are more,
much more, than two sloughed off from thirty-eight.
When I find I've driven you, thoughtlessly,
near his home—until so lately second to your own—
I know (though I watch the road ahead)
you have turned to stare with the hope
that hope could render change.
I think of trying to speak of time,
easing, and endurance. But truth would lead
to the girl I lived for twenty years ago,
to the drive I always take—each summer,
each Christmas—eight hundred miles from here,
a few miles off from my parents' home.

Metamorphosis is real for all of us,
and not only in our daily mirrors:
The girl has *become* that house I pass and pass
those days, feeling as if night is leaning in,
as if my travels are the final point
in logic's proof of total foolishness.
But still I ride that long, slow hill, ticking
through every block, past each cornered street sign
with its letters raised and painted and piked.
And then 261: the round door window,
the three porch pillars, the seven steps,
the twenty years of my stomach's falling
to this other place where we ride so close
in sorrow and, therefore, ride apart.

The Tempest

—for my daughter Miranda

If you name your daughter *vision*,
or *wondrous to behold*, you should not be surprised
if she comes to you in anger or in shame,
wishing to be known as *Mary* or *Ann*.
That will be the moment to carry her out
to the things of the world she is not,
speaking other sounds that were almost hers:
Aspen, lily-white, cumulonimbus glow.

Soon enough she'll realize the world,
too often, gets named in hope of profit,
or deceit, or the scientist's exactitude.
But on the greening island of the family
testing its voice in the months of waiting,
the sought-after words are music and the past:
Grandparent. Aunt. Child deceased.

Spirits of fashion and monsters of commerce
lurk, bedfellows eager to keep us
from our own best inventions and songs.
Some days it seems we grow from wailing silence
into speech, only that we might curse
the coming return to silence.
But if you've named your daughter *wondrous to behold*,
she'll someday learn she heard those words
before all others, and then again, and again.
When you are gone beyond all roaring
she'll know, should you ever brave return,
which words are the first you'll speak.

IV. *Remoldings*

Redundancies

So we move to moisten
what is already damp,
to wet what is already moist.

Shadows in hand,
we trace the traced.

What is hot we heat—
what is open, open wide—
what is filled fill again,
spill over, and fill.

The risen we raise,
the plumbed we sound.

Already posed,
the positions hold—
what was there
is there once more.

He Defines *Definition*

Start from nothing.
                    Add the woman's body
beside you on the bed, naked outline
black on the window's light, hip the fulcrum
for a balance that might be dream.
                              Drop
the illusion of clarity, the lens
you had thought that the heart might become.

As she stays on her side, supply her arm
lifting above her head, raising muscle
in a rounded line from armpit to waist.

Consider photographs—the unreal focus
their slick paper statements provide,
the way they can drill across space—
broadcasting invisible seen, reforming intact.

Start again.
              She is still beside you.
Still the blur of uncountable movements
barely encased by a skin
of fixed moment.
                    Still the word, waiting.

Cast

"Does spelling count?" the students ask,
and I know they have lost
the wisdom of magic: the miraculous arising
from the cruelly exact—the hordes of wizards' brooms
advancing, and only one sound in all the world
to save us from collapse.

Words are plain and *gray*, are plain and *grey*,
and two worlds open to sight:

Gray is the crayons of children,
the hair of pioneer women,
the clouds churning above the plain
rumbled by an endless stampede.

Grey is the stone of the manor house,
the thick but wisping fogs,
the sleek, horrific ghosts over the fens.

Tom and *Tim*, *Jan* and *Jane*—countries
cast or broken by a letter's mold,
the *yea* or *nay* of the heart.

Inventing the Black Bees of Love

Black bees could be the heart
for any beginning we make.
Their sound says, "Never listen
to the silence others demand.
Listen only to the hot raging
we offer, the melting closed of all ears
when a tongue makes its mark on skin."

Black bees could be the tight-wound hairs
we loosen, cores unrolling outward
in swarms of wiry thread—
our bodies standing forth to prove
no reason, no thinking out or holding back,
can cover up or force aside
the damp and fiery combs.

Poppy Field Near Giverny

Year upon year the great paintings hang
as if finally home, like crown jewels or corpses.
They counsel patience and fearlessness—
in our standing before them, in our watching
the world through the rest of our lives.
Just so, glowing poppies remain in Boston
where once they asked me the words for light
they gave to our hands as we paused, then passed.
These poppies, more patient than I with the silence
our years have brought, trust that now is the good
ripe time for breaking through—though I break
all rules of decorum by telling
the fact of flowers talking,
their voices clear as the dangerous
clicks from the Geiger counter's tube.

Who can doubt that Monet prepared for us alone
throughout his years of shifting vision,
casting anew his own home's countryside—
knowing we would come to this rising flat of orange,
its aura an inviting double swath
in the shallow trough of grassy hills.
Monet, so delicately wise to the tricks
the twins of time and light will play,
would look without surprise at our blending
into his clear obsessions with lover and place.
We even preceded him, coolly stretching
our hopes on the ground as model
for his painterly, all-receptive eye:
he drew from us soft slopings, color,
quiet, the twinge of emptiness.

Here is an Earth where sky is pointless,
a center that needs no boundary—

here the burning ground of fallen angels,
the open skin of the grave announcing
how the Earth is flowers, down and down.

The poppies thin at the foreground,
their sparseness moving straight
toward where we stand today,
the ragtag tail of a history.

I've not yet spoken of lying down
to make our bodies wet and otherworldly
on this bed too perfect to deserve,
have not paraded the ways we might be fired.
So let me end the coyness now
since finally there are no privacies,
if only because we constantly pray to give
our deepest thoughts and feelings to the air:
this painting is nothing if not a bed
to fuel erotic hopes, that they might fuel
all others.
        Art begins with the body
and ends with the body. We reach the jinni
with our hands, the live stroking the lifeless
to draw forth what was and was not there before.
Then, having found the huge but simple power,
we turn to it as often as we can—
though learning, as we must, how every touch increases
the jinni's strength to serve us,
and its need to break away.

Reasons for Love

Greasy bones are passion's proof
in ways we deny and deny
by hiding each day's denial.
The butcher's barrel is reason for love.
The rotting of fruit is sweet,
of grains and cheeses sour,
of flesh repulsive.

The whetstone's honing can chill,
not with its grinding and whine,
but with renewal it refuses to us:
only dead bones can be sharpened.

Greasy bones demand our love,
our fingers coated at this feast
whose meat, uncooked, would rot—
cooked and uneaten, would rot—
left alive in the fields, would rot.
My finger at your neck, trailing down
into your open blouse, undeniable
snail's track of glistening grease
rising onto your breast.
As I reach your nipple,
the fat of the animal nearly gone
from my fingertip, a final pressure
yields a last, faint smear to shine
the rough-soft mesa of brown.

Sovereigns of contradiction, we know
the demand of fate, the fate of demand:
your hand at my cheek, my face
to your breast—one light tongue-stroke
to taste and clean and clear,
our cart wheeling and wheeling
over the bones of the dead.

Halves of Houses

That day, we saw how what goes up need not come down,
how the sound of one hand clapping might be something
akin to a roof with half a peak. Far out
on a country road, between an empty village
and an almost empty town, we met two halves of houses,
one a quarter mile behind the other,
trundling toward us in a flap of banners
proclaiming , in yellow and red, *Wide Load*.

We eased out near our shoulder, evading
those two stark edges that overhung the center,
wobbling, offering to shear us off.
Inside our gradual swerving
we leaned even more to the right,
as if taking some action with our bodies
might save us though the car were crushed.

Yet, really, we scarcely thought of those two bulks passing,
took them in stride like a cough or a shooting pain.
Only when a second brace lurched by, and a third,
was I touched by the sense of another world,
one where houses are constantly sliced apart
or waiting to be spliced together—
though in either case sent packing on display
so folks of every age might pause and point:
"*There* is where the heart is," one might say,
or another, "There's no place like *that*."

The clean-cut pairs kept rolling on with the miles—
ten, a dozen, fifteen or more. Tremendous
black plastic sheets across each opening
prevented our seeing whatever might have been
inside: cutaway doll-house scenes, everything
in place, complete and angled our way?

Flipped-about carnage of furnishings and bodies?
Emptiness parceled into rooms, each with its little
proscenium arch, each ready for the nailing
together, the sealing of flimsy symmetry
ripe for tornadoes and floods?

What else we had always thought solid
might suddenly appear on these roads
we know far better than our own minds?
Maybe the cathedral of Notre Dame,
worshippers spilling out onto the pavement,
the cockeyed altar splitting like a wishbone.
Behind that, perhaps, our parents lopped
like sides of aging beef.

Some wholes are useless.
In the jungle, the machete
thunks the hairy rock of the cocoanut
to lay forth sweetest smell, and drink, and food.
The circle and its breathed-full relative, the sphere,
remind us of completion and harmony,
yet always we have worked on the science of division:
degrees, minutes, and seconds of the circle's plane,
or the sphere's invisible units framed
by the leaps of inductive calculus.

You did in fact lean outward with me
at the first, fearing a real collision.
But all this other, the high-flown
cabbages and kings . . .
in your blink and yawn I saw

we had gathered no greatness
from this drive together.

Like is a free ride, a lark, compared with *is*.

All this talk is mine. All this metaphor
struggles to stay afloat in our wordlessness,
your perpetual gaze out the passenger's window.

Flying through Gold

Do you tire of the preaching of words,
allegorical sheening of loss?
Look to your own heart,
its chambers of black and red.

*

A finger takes flight,
gliding through the simple ring
to a life, bursting air to acquire
a hard and permanent clothing.

This is to say
the instant of wedding is steel
we would bolt to the rockface,
is the delicate clocks we would break.

*

Gold leaf is stamped and sunken by hand
into the Bible's front and spine.
The bride held the book at the altar,
lays it forever beside the bed.

The more it is touched, the quicker
the gilt work cracks and flakes away.

*

There is also the locket,
tiny casket around the neck
given only to women and girls.
The spirits wing forth from the throat
without warning, hang their oval faces
in the daily air before us—
inviting our touch, demanding their place.

*

A king lived by gold and died by gold—
poured molten down his gullet by councilors.
You must take this as you will, conjuring
tales of his final thoughts or words or sounds.

*

After pain and decay, the body becomes gold.
We become the last hope of desperate men:
our skeletons discovered deep in woods,
our gleaming grin a cave to be mined
a mere foot north of the missing heart.

Complicated Shadows

To hawks we're a woodland insect,
four legs above and four below, twitching
on the ground as if a flash-tongued sun
sought to flicker through us to the spot we've claimed.

Each small move we make is shading for one,
quick burning for the other—our bodies
become one another's clothing tugged off,
wrapped on, stripped away again in glowing haste.

The question of shadows gains depth
when our stomachs press close
to leave no space from skin to skin,
sealing a damp plane between us,
a pressure of pure darkness
we feel but cannot see:
light needs at least a chance to be absent—
no shadows in locked closets,
behind closed lids, within the heart's chambers.

We are weaving and folding, we
know this soil is a great compost heap,
we are making and unmaking
light—forcing the aging hot sun to run.

Hunger

We lost ourselves in the caves,
the homes, that our mouths could be.
Knowing the kiss was invented,
we let ourselves be the ancient flesh
first in the world to make that move:

> We were panting in scraggly underbrush,
> hidden after hours of running
> scarcely ahead of hatred and clubs.
> One body atop the other
> in the thorn thicket's narrow reprieve,
> we were the neural spark toward survival—
> pressing our lips to silence breath.

> Next, *we* were the enemies
> grappling, pinned and breaking and locked again.
> You clamped me down spread-eagled,
> I tried to scream for help, you
> cut me short with the only weapon left.

> We were deformed, handless neighbors
> fighting for rights to a berry bush,
> turning teeth upon each other
> but drawn to the way juice leaked
> back and forth—clashing and feeding confused
> till soon we were stripping branches
> together, tongues lifting the sweetness
> from here to there, and back.

> We were crippled desert companions
> abandoned to burn at oasis' edge:
> I scooched and strained to the water,
> carried strength back in my mouth to you.

Rapt by sounds and their source,
we sought—like gaming children
  · gleefully lifting shirts and pressing navels—
to make our noises flush with one another.

And through it all we were history,
keenly making the already made.
We were Dracula at throat, baby at breast—
were throat and breast, were givers and takers
awed by the endless need for hunger.

Making the Mouth

The tongue takes its many shapes
quick-sung with soft exactitude:
the drawing back and down of *H*,
the upward flick of *L*—
that sweet snail of thought made flesh
all pink-red on the move
to leave its winding trail
on one ground or another.

To taste and speak are twins—
the flavor of a human voice,
the electric verb of tongue on salty skin—
between them making the mouth's old tenant
a matter of survival:
prehensile muscle
dropping slack for *A*,
rising to tautness for *Z*;
building a fire with moisture,
a moan with soft vibrations,
the corpus of a language
through countless nimble shiftings.

The tongue is the body's mockingbird
from infancy onward, turning for nourishment
first to what it needs, then to all
it wants to know, then to what it loves,
last to what if fears and cries against.;

yet the tongue is the body's gazelle,
springing and springing
to cover the veldt's expanse,
to rise above its dangers
by almost never touching down;

yet the tongue is the body's nightingale—
light and shadow, straight and crooked,
sound and silence, before and after—
filling the mouth
or fulfilling its emptiness;

yet the tongue is the body's shark,
whose cessation of movement is death.

Taking the Light Whitely

Certain habits can seem miraculous
in the thoughts of the dispossessed:
to have chosen your own clothing
from stores and then your closet,
to have shaven yet again in the mist
dulling your bathroom mirror—
such are the dreams of the homeless . . . .

I rarely consider my fingers or tongue
until slicing or slamming or burning.
Now, I see how the air outlines the air
in every space where you're not.
I see how we let the ways we caressed
mound like seeds in a bushel basket,
uniform, topping off higher and higher
for as long as we could pour.
I see all those mornings by windows,
on beds nearly overflowing
with movements we made and made, and felt
we watched more closely than we did.
Now we are a history I work to imagine
into every place we were, a chronicle
no others could even think to restore.
And we are a future, scattered across the country
in the separate strings of houses
we will come to occupy with others—
some for many years.
We do not know them yet, there is nothing
familiar in their rooms or air.
And still, each holds today
what will hold when we've come and gone:
shafts of sun on a thin sill, a pine floor,
a stark wall of whatever color—
one space after another

taking the light whitely,
spot after spot illumined
by that which must touch without touching.

Writer

In this job I need not worry
the stone of my body's weakening.
No fear that in a year, or two, or three,
the spine will grate and the muscles thin,
leaving too many boxes too long
on wharf or truck or shelf. No losing
one's eye for the curveball's coming, one's touch
for incision to stop the heart's infarction.

In this job the office never blows apart,
the load never shifts to sever a leg
or send a buddy's skull to heaven
in a plastic bag. Nothing leaks heat,
or cold, or worse, to the marrow.

In this job my body is mine.
No legs open and mounted
for a buck or a fix, no small child
hungry at home until I take the world
into my mouth, no whips or shouting
to hunch my naked shoulders.

Here, I need not wonder
what a job might be. No tunneling, icy winds
down alleys toward ears and forehead.
No crouching in African dust, lolling
with flies at my nose and lips.

In this job I am trying to learn
which role is mine in the Wonderland
Party: the March Hare, telling Alice
"Take some more tea"? Or Alice,
replying, "I've had nothing yet, so
I can't take more"? Or the Mad Hatter, shrieking

"You mean you can't take less.
It's easy to take *more* than nothing."
Or the Dormouse, so sincere,
swearing to the others
he's heard every word they were saying,
then trying to tell his story
before he drifts back into sleep.

from

There Is No Finished World

(2003)

Knotter

n. 1. a person or thing that ties knots   2. a remover of knots

Henceforth I shall be the one
preparing strips of inflammable cloth,
wrapping pole torches that they might yield
an incandescent light, hours-long, to every needy moth.

Or perhaps I'll back up farther,
will be the one breaking down
the gnarled pine-pitch torches, raveling
flammable wood strands to soak
in viscous resin for slow, candescent burning.

And then there's that old magician
I might be, with his elementary trick:
those complicated loopings-through of rope
followed by that double-handed outward snap
you expect will bulk the knot up tight—
yet suddenly off it flows, water over rock,
leaving a pure straight line of twisted threads
old Karl Wallenda's ghost could dance across,
a horizon soft spring sun might lift above.

Understand

Forgetting Mortality

It's our job—while flipping burgers or turning
potters' wheels or tuning Ferraris—and
it's what we must do well or not at all:
no "sort of thinking of my death today" will do,
nor half-assed notions that your ass will soon be grass.
Be it day or swing or graveyard—what's in a name?—
every shift is one we're ready to take, one
we'll show up for, gripe about, and float through
till they set us loose or toss us out.
Over yonder's the unemployment line,
the one we'll all clock into down the road.
For now, we're working at the this-then-that-then-
this-again—a cycle sometimes the seconds
of an assembly line, sometimes the years
between inventive thoughts.
                        But all of it is,
as they say—this pumping gas, this
opening and closing of the heart, this
pounding of the beat with stick and gun—
a living.

Employment

I have a friend I have not seen
these dozen years or more, a man without his rightful work
because no job existed in America, not one,
for a Doctor of Philosophy
in Philosophy of Religion.
Just months before our final meeting
he'd read and thought and written
his way at last to that degree,
then found himself dead
center in the garish spotlight
suffered by Woody Allen's Liam Beamish,
who "could remove his false teeth and eat peanut brittle,
which he did every day for sixteen years
until someone told him there was no such profession."

Sporting the smooth élan of a stand-up comic
while his toddlers swarmed around him and the TV blared,
my friend would quick-talk tales of the world's bizarre believers:
the ascetic Pakistani hermit, living with arm outstretched
for years until it froze there, atrophied;
the famous grazing monks of Medieval France,
who approached Nature and God each morning
through a reverent, extended munching of the monastery grounds.

That last afternoon, we escaped upstairs to his bedroom
like eight-year-olds on the lam from a grown-ups' party.
He dug from his underwear drawer the prize
flea-market find his wife (they've since divorced)
would never let him hang, nor even speak of in her presence:
inside an overlarge, gilded wooden frame,
peering through twenty-odd ovals
trimmed from a once-white mat,
the tight-tuxedoed necks and dour looks
glued on the faces of the Class of 1949,
Castleman School of Mortuary Science.

I still recall our lunatic remarks
addressed to those clean-shaven baby men
who'd already touched more dead than I would ever see,
who'd stood long-robed and marched in line
across some creaking stage to proclaim their skills with death.
All that we said soon left us
sprawled in hysterics on the double bed
as we spun out endless histories, past and future,
for the stalwart Castleman clan gone forth
in the year of Orwell's *1984*:
One became Chief Embalmer
for Persians and poodles and cockatiels
entombed at LA's Petland Heaven,
another left the business and street-hawked Oil of Olay
in the bench-filled parks of St. Petersburg, Fla.

He *did* find a job, of course,
and likely has it still,
counseling mothers and fathers
against beating their children.
His every word and look and hand through the air
might be fuel as easily as water—
another infant flipped against a wall.
It's never what we're trained for.
It's what we find, and make of it, and live with.

A String Around Your Finger

We forget so as not to be reminded
we used up such-and-such a time
doing this or that, spent twice as long
focused completely on that thing there
when we'd better have so-on-and-so-forth . . .

We cringe with delight at the weird
statistics surfacing here and there:
in a year we down seventeen pounds of sugar—
in a decade drink twenty-nine barrels of water—
the typical male, in a lifetime,
ejaculates two or three gallons.

What's done seems done, including all the tricks
baked into the language pie, if only we'd listen.
I'm well past forty now—can someone, please,
tell me the meaning of *hellbent for leather*?

The Great Mandala circles only once for each of us,
the wheel of fortune several times at best—
though some of us learn to spin
through untold revolutions
on our bodies' own thin axes
while we creak and grind along.

Some words break the rhythm of every line
you'd think to work them into: orgasm
is one of this ilk, leaving us lurching every time.
Do you recall your first, the way it split
your past and present like a ten-foot wall?
(*There's* a man's question, she'll say.)

As I said, we'd never forget a thing
if we lived forever. All threats would be dead,
and all fears, so our burst-proof brains could fill
and fill until the cows came home and all the angels sang.

"Walk-Ins Welcome"

To go without appointment is the only hope.
Arrive when expected, by agreement,
and you're treated to be sent away—
your time comes, your time is done and gone.
Come randomly, uncalled for, and your prospects
multiply. You might be turned away—
"Yes, we know what the sign says,
but today is just impossible"—
or you might be embraced, grudgingly
or dearly. You might be ushered in
pronto, hair to be trimmed or infection staunched,
or you might sit waiting among the crowds
of the signed-up and others like yourself.
When finally called, you might be overcome
by gratefulness or exasperation, and
you might be greeted by the same on the other side
of the perennial curtain or door.
When you leave—improved or not,
helped or not, repaired or not—
you need not feel the end is here
nor feel you must be gone for weeks
or months until your time comes round again.
you can click the door behind you,
turn to stare up at the still-lighted sign,
and walk back in.

What I Don't Understand

I had thought to begin with telephones,
how I heard this morning in Georgia
a woman's voice, clearly and simply, from southern France—
but I've decided now to start with lint
as it is gathered by the sack-full in South Carolina,
bagged by many from the region's washing machines
and bought by one to be transformed into art:
lint sculpture sometimes, but usually lint collage
on paper, or lint mixed with paints on canvas or wood.

A grocery list is not a poem,
so I cannot hope to hold you here
endlessly rocked from page to page
in some high-falutin' litany
à la Sears & Roebuck or L. L. Bean;
we must have some development,
if only toward the obsolete
senses of *understand*: to prop up or support;
to know how to conduct oneself in proper form.

In high school chemistry we gathered words
to paste upon our brains as we watched
the shifts of color and state in tubes and beakers:
Valence, bonding, molar and of course *molal,*
the *asymptote* toward *absolute zero.*
I carry these now in my head in the trusting way
I keep and peruse at night my senior annual,
block after block of faces and names
a quarter-century gone into versions
of whatever it is I've gone to myself.
Victoria Calamucci. David and Daniel
Christopherson. Jane Dale. Beverly Dawn
Fratelli. Beverley Jean Giroux.

Universe

The one turning is all we seek:
a warm noon breeze at winter's end,
the child's fever breaking in time,
the single pair of eyes our way
in the overcrowded room—
their depth-gaze proclaiming
we are, beyond all doubt,
the one. Turning is all we seek:
butter from milk, hawk in gyre,
leaf in whirlpool, steel from fire,
many strong backs against violence and war,
old prejudice into respect for
the one turning. Is all we seek
a shift in sameness, the grave's precursor
Poe saw daily in his canted mirror?
Or do we wish for change like God's, all
revolving and evolving within the great bubble
the one turning is? All we seek
drives us to question the sought—
what worth this canvas daubed with paint,
this debit to the ledger, this rush of blood
in bed or birth or slaughter?
How long can we move ourselves to believe
the one turning is all? We seek
the change that does not mean the end—
aloneness into love, dullness to arousal,
flat brown fields to gauze of sprouting green—
the change that primes and perks us
for the world, mutes the narrow notion
the one turning is all *we*. Seek
and ye shall seek—*there's* a turn
that turns a phrase our way.
We have pancakes and pirouettes,
Satan's anus-gate to heaven,

hot to cold, elation to despair,
rock to lava to rock.
We have the child's first smile, first step, first word.
And everywhere we look we look, and
the one turning is all we seek.

from *Poems of This Size*

Poems of This Size

In poems of this size, so little
might happen, one wonders if such brevity
can matter—as when I strolled, thirty years ago,
with my wife (a year before she was my wife)
in her first neighborhood, and we heard
that familiar, horrible squealing of tires down the block.
And because she was a young nurse, no doctor
in sight, when we reached the small boy
lying on the red-brick street with many people
gathered around, *she* had to step forward and kneel,
had to be the one cradling him and wondering,
most closely, at how quick and full an end can be.

Carpe Diem

I want the mind of Emerson
at the moment of his first masturbation,
Dickinson faced with the bloody cloth,
all the genius children of the world
when their bodies grabbed their throats
and squeezed into silence those beautifully windy brains.

The Boy Scout's Motto Explodes

No matter all the myths of departure
and return, all of nature's taut cycles,
all holidays and anniversaries
through my full half-century of breathing
in and out, quick and slow, deep and shallow,
still there's no name for my daughter's breast milk
bottled in my hand, this nourishment expressed
for my grandson's delight and survival
in my arms while she is absent—she to be known
soon to him as Mother, she I once knew
as a sleeping white cocoon of blanket
beside *her* mother—whose then-hard breast I tongued
to give relief and, it seems today, to prompt a world.

Editing Poems During a Hospital Deathwatch

Dear Poet:

I'm sorry, but I couldn't use your art
today to soothe or distract me from this death—
not quite accomplished yet, but pressing out
as twitchings of her cold and curling feet,
as ulcerous brown blood seeping with her breath.
I expect, had you known, you might have sent
something more attuned to the current path
my mother-in-law is facing. I'm sure
you're thinking this private critique unfair,
and you'd be right to be upset, except
that you'd be wrong. This place, right here, is where
we *always* meet: Beatrice with her chart
devoid of final blessings, you and I
Searching for the words that nail sensation to the sky.

Measures

Measures

I knew a woman
who wouldn't trust a man
who wouldn't eat zucchini plain—
something about simplicity,
readiness to live far down
the line from blood and thundering.

The oddest measures
have ways of ensuring
truth is wrung from complexity,
she said. No lies with zucchini,
she said. And no preening. No murders.

Her angora, purring,
would sprawl its silken fur
across us both, limply—
chest on my thigh, belly on hers.
In all the muscles, such serenity.

Bobcat, lynx, cougar, lion—
all, of course, were *kitten*
once, she said. That's given.
And a man's eye when he sees them,
or hears that word—she'd know him then.

Living Hands

        —See, here it is—
        I hold it towards you

They stood, sides touching, and stared at the hand of Keats
open to them there behind the glass, its movements a map
inscribing what otherwise none (save John) could sense:
the pulsings and shiftings of the only brain ever
to form the strange and massive shell, *Endymion*,
now thus beached before these two by countless quirks of histories.

We, the knowing watchers of these lookers, must wonder
how their own felt thoughts, on beauty or art or death, might differ
had not the couple just an hour (or two) ago been making love
with a wired intensity long unfamiliar to both—
so that while they gaped at that ink two centuries old,
that paper more durable not only than flesh but than bone,
her body leaked their moisture into her clothing
and the dampness of his still tingled
while thick crowds milled and paused throughout
the Romantic exhibit, with its cluster of clear enclosures
showing off the passionate hands of so many
to the eyes of so many more.

And that could be the ending to the story, that "more,"
and you out there might turn away to think nine hundred things,
perhaps among them these:

      Will there never be an end to poems invoking Keats?

      I was, I must admit, slightly arouse by those later lines.

      Is that "they" a transparent screen for "we,"
      or did the poet observe and conjure—or conjure whole?

What you could not think to ask was whether, as I wrote,
a woman—unexpected—came to me with a warm and scented cloth
which I might press against my hands and face and neck,
thus bringing me back from body-in-mind to body
while the darkened ocean rolled backwards beneath me, six miles down
below our jumbo jet aimed toward a country I'd never seen—
and where I'd set forth to alter my life

in ways this poem has no chance of encompassing.
But I'm telling you she did,, and though I've never seen her again,
she helped me to know what I must have sensed already: the tale
could not be finished, since no satisfactory story
encompassing stone lions could possibly end without those lions
ever coming to the page.

Of course: the statues outside the exhibition hall,
ones the lovers did not think twice about, or so the man would have said
if asked before the woman's letter came some weeks beyond that day—
the letter that said she knew, or felt she knew, he hadn't known
the lengths to which her body would have gone that afternoon,
         that moment
when she pressed her hip to his and read

            . . . we will shade
    Ourselves whole summers by a river glade;
    And I will tell thee stories of the sky,
    And breathe thee whispers of its minstrelsy.

She would, she said, have fucked him at that moment on those lions,
either or both, and no need to clear the crowds away.

→

And so, having sworn he'd always trust her,
he entered a life that had at least one reality
he felt as more fantastic than his fantasies;
at oddest moments he would enter that truth, to picture
her seated, naked, on the narrow ledge by a lion's crouched legs.
He lifted the crooks of his elbows into those of her knees
to raise her, while she reached out to clutch him,
to pull him toward and into her, and all
the while the crowds might have *their* wills, too—
for those others did not, could not, matter.

I have no proof, as always, but something tells me
it's more than accident that broke this poem in half,
that left me stranded for weeks on that harsh word, *fuck*,
and wouldn't free us all into what has followed
until I took to the air again, bound that time
for a nearer and far less curious city—though one,
I'd learned, where I'd likely encounter a woman
lost to my life for more than a decade, a woman
who had proven for me then, if anyone could, this anecdote
I'd later heard of the lion letter might be true.

No, I've got no stories to tell of that woman.
Rather, now might be the time to take more questions,
or to bring back that long-stranded, still-pulsing
hand of Keats, as if *it* held the answers
we want—or pretend—to seek. But in fact there's nothing left,
not even the time-warp tale I once set forth into plotting:

In that one, a poet without belief beheld an angel
who offered him the chance to sacrifice his life
to bring Keats back to breathe and write
for three-score-years-and-ten, or more.
That agnostic poet paused, trying to imagine what Keats could write

in the shadow of the year 2000, or whether he'd write at all.
Staring at the angel, unable to answer its question
on his own, he knew for the first time in his life
that whatever he did would be equally—absolutely—right
and wrong. Finally, in this story that never quite existed,
he closed and clenched his fists, and closed his eyes to the angel.

1998: One Hundred Years Together

—for Mary

We are a century now—and though
the merest far-cry shadow to my grandpa,
who'll next year be his own 100,
our whole of equal parts is still
a source for me of, frankly, wonder.
Alone, I would be merely fifty,
yourself unlinked the same—
just fifty-fifty, just two wandering I's
left to chance, to this-or-that, to
eggless ham and yinless yang.

Our quartet of daughters—the numbers cannot lie—
add up this very year to a full life lived:
twenty-eight, twenty-five, eleven, and six
make the infamous three-score and ten.
There is not quite a symbol here,
not quite a meaning for the ages—
but, at the least, another moment's lesson:
anniversaries are such as we declare.
Our infants' ages we declaim in days at first,
then weeks and months and then half-years
before we settle for the sun's demanding
circuit, trimming our allotment back and back.

My dear, recall there was only a single day
in our 18,000-plus apiece
when we'd made love just once together:
before that one day, never;
the next, the count continued.

In American deserts the century plant
blooms once and dies—but the flower comes
after ten to thirty years. Was it named
by someone stupid, impatient, or wise?
Who could have been there at the breaking through
from the crust of rocky sand, then settled in
for the seemingly endless growth
and maturing of the nameless *agave*?
Who could have held that chain of days
together with no knowing where
or to what it all might lead?

Yet here we are, one hundred together
by a count we'll let none put asunder.
Agave means illustrious,
versary turning, *anni* a year at a time.
We must learn when to let things wander,
learn when to make them rhyme.

Who Would Not Seek the Perfect Gesture of Love?

Never was there anything enough to say . . .
yet once there I was,
watching the back of your head
and the left side of your jaw line
from my seat behind you on the crowded bus
as you gazed out the window,
there in that time when I was
brought into your presence, by our work
and by chance, for a week after years
apart, years of what they call *nothing*,
but of course was unable to touch you
since I had no rights in the world
outside of our fractured hearts—
and as I watched, a stray blacksilver hair
waved and swayed apart from the rest,
a cracked limb dangling in wind
like the wand of a fairy or the scepter of a priest
offering its foreign blessing
to one who dares approach.

I reached over the seat back; you still stared
away. My hand passed above your right
shoulder and alongside your neck,
opposite the window. I caught the thread
(younger and smarter I'd have called it *angelic*)
in the pincer of two empty fingers
to lift it away—a tiny blemish,
a flaw that could float on air.

Mortal Fathers and Daughters

Anything

—for Catherine

"Do you file your nails?"
"Why . . . yes."
"Some people will save anything."
[one of Uncle Jim's old jokes]

How about this small square napkin,
in my lap five miles from the Earth
as we hum toward Lima to adopt an infant girl
we've never seen, or even heard described?
Might there be enshrinement in the air
this moment, in the American Airlines double-A imprinted
between thick bars extending across the delicate paper?
Crumpled and abandoned, it's gone within days
to landfill or burning; properly covered and laid away,
thinner than eyelid or veil,
it's somewhere intact when I am gone to bone.

I, not one who weeps, would weep
one day, I'm sure—not for a napkin
perhaps, but certainly for strands of hair
taped down in a scrapbook beside it: hair of Catherine,
invisible child-to-be, or of the older others,
three more daughters and a single wife.
Or even hairs I might not recognize,
through fault of sight or memory,
and perhaps they'd be something else entirely—
say, garment threads of black and brown
coiling upon themselves and offering
no hints to where they came from, but only
what we'd know already: that everything
pressed and preserved on these pages

turns to emblem, has no hope of ever being
itself again.

                I am past the danger point here,
launched into sentiment I see
no way to funnel out of easily.
Of course, there is that element I missed
in my napkin logo, those geometric wings
close above the double *A* trapezoids
angled so the one behind is broken,
its tiny lower tip jutting at the left—an eagle's tail—
and the bottom of the front one is notched
to be the stretched-forth talons in descent.
Perhaps we might save these wings alone,
trim them free with moustache scissors
like a photo cut down for a locket,
then tape them down dead-center of an album sheet—
there to be found some year and compared,
in their crossing, to the perfect fingers
an oblivious newborn waggles in her sleep,
or the countless sets of woven veins
in the electric muscle of the heart—
that lives its lifetime buried,
that we only dream of bringing into light.

Death Tricks

Because we give the earth our dead, we believe
it can hold anything.
Burial equals gone: father or nuclear waste,
we watch it go down, then turn away
to stay alive. I watched my fingers putrefy
as they lay on my thigh one full-moon night
while I sat on my back porch steps;
my flesh gave off that smell I've never smelled,
the one police describe as the thing
you can never imagine beforehand.

Thousands lie drugged and dying
in the carpetless rooms of city streets,
others grow deeply and lastingly rich
shaping perfect replicas of gun-shot faces
to be filmed for our viewing pleasure.

My father's corpse at my back, I chatted
with friends and a few strangers—
this is called *condolence*, from the Latin
condolens, "to suffer with"—
until my daughter, twelve years old,
asked where his stomach had gone.
And of course she was right:
already they were changing the story,
taking him from us—already
he was younger, sleek for the flight.

My Daughter Playing Beethoven on My Chest

—for Rebecca

She was nine, on the absolute edge
between her dying childhood and
that confusing ecstasy to come
then go in another decade's rush.

We were simply chattering—I
seated and she standing before me, she
spinning those silly child's nonsense tales
still lingering, circular repeating
jabberings a part of me laughs and loves
to hear, though often I am quickly bored,
annoyed, wishing to escape the wishing
her fantasy of words and voices means—
when suddenly her hands came forward and up,
spreading like claws or the reach of a smaller child
playing ghosts or monsters. But her fingers kept coming
and lit upon my chest, ever so briefly
still, then launched into a spidery dance
of side to side, of up and down—
Beethoven's "Ode to Joy" thrummed above my lungs
as if she were typing out a secret
well-known message.   No, I could not decipher
that music's motion, upside-down and silent.
She hummed as well, her fully childish voice
releasing that long-ago tale of maturity,
as if it were the simplest thing of all
to offer up the musings of a genius.

What she played I could not play,
my hands from earliest days fat hams

stuck to the platter of my thinking,
music's flags and circles a Russian I could not read.
But I'd had ear enough to follow
the lead of her growing fingers—
at seven, then eight, then nine—on the keys,
which led to hammers and wires and board,
which had lifted sound through our every room and wall.

Notes from the Year of My Father's Dying

It's one thing to be clever about death,
as in tossing off the notion that you wear it
every day around your wrist. It's something else
to wake and be wearing it there.

*

What the blueprints fail to show is the slum
this beautiful home, unbuilt, will become.

*

I am four or five when my father proposes
a weeks-long reading of mysterious tales
whose inhabitants' very names are wonder:
Mowgli, Shere-Khan. I am ready
for each night's fragment, live
in full belief that tomorrow's piece
will be perfectly trailed by the next . . .

*

Stunning what little we'll hold of a life
and think we're somewhere near it.

*

And what is the answer from shower-stall tiles,
the fine ivory lines of grouting
beaded with water and perfect as health?
Slowly, you wash your body for the dead
one who is out there waiting.

*

. . . it will tear
our eyes and lips to the very end.

*

Watch unstrapped and squeezed in hand, I'm the boy
in the back seat in contest with himself,
holding his breath in the hot wind's roaring
while his family hurtles on without knowing
I have ceased, for now, the act of life.

*

Now the Earth fills with the known,
mystery dissolved by monogrammed gold:
the tie tack with its gothic letters, DBC,
clasped and clasped by the dark vacuum.

*

And then there is nothing but death
as we suddenly learn of the masks
the middle-aged had worn when we were children,
showing us ease and comfort we took for real.

*

We must have a code
for the time when silence comes.

Called Forward

Dale B. Corey, 1925–1985
Emily Dickinson, 1830–1886

Other poets to my father's grave
most certainly have never come;
to Dickinson's Amherst kingdom,
iron-fenced, they've trudged in iambic waves.
And so I owe my poem to him—
yet pay it now to her, most fierce
in genius, cold and warm and sparse,
who speaks above his silent din.
She saw his face and bones, born then gone
century and century beyond her;
she spoke his love, his chill, his stupor—
she taught me *grief is tongueless*, gave me song.

My Daughters' Photograph as a Bookmark in *Howl*

All I have at hand for the long flight,
dug from my book-filled backpack it becomes
the marker for this chapter in my life of reading:
These four together—two women, two girls—
with twenty-one years between oldest and babe,
all primmed and posed and primed for the eldest's wedding.

> *angelheaded hipsters burning for the ancient heavenly*
> *connection . . .*

Their backdrop the deep false blue so favored
by gallant commercial photographers,
this is the endless array of our daughters:
twenty-four, twenty-one, seven, and three,
skins from cherubic Swedish pink to Asian
olive to Andean mestizo brown.

> *who wandered around and around at midnight in the*
> *railroad yard wondering where to go, and went,*
> *leaving no broken hearts . . .*

Surrounding this chemical miracle
rolled moments and hours not to be lost
on the older two until infirmity:
Heather the bride, with rights to this day
as its shining center, this one day
when all would turn and stand and nearly bow,
this day when the heavy wooden doors
and the stained-glass windows of perception are cleansed;
Miranda the honored maid, caught by the web of the past

→

and the mirror of the future at once,
forced to turn away in tears when the aisle filled
with her familiar sister's radiance.

> *who cut their wrists three times successively unsuccess-*
>   *fully, gave up and were forced to open antique*
>   *stores where they thought they were growing*
>   *old and cried . . .*

This portrait that will surprise the younger two
in years to come, their flourishing brain cells
ripe at three and seven for permanent filing
(until infirmity) of words and inflections and sentences,
of spellings and plots and processes and arcane detail,
but not yet ready to hold the larger events
so laden, we'll tell them later, with something
we call significance, the parent of nostalgia.

> *Moloch! Solitude! Filth! Ugliness! Ashcans and unob-*
>   *tainable dollars! Children screaming under the*
>   *stairways! Boys sobbing in armies! Old men*
>   *weeping in the parks!*

This famous *Howl* I hold is worlds
these women/girls will likely never know—
world of ecstatic suffering,
world of suffering made ecstatic art—
for they are not bound toward impoverished dissolution,
nor likely to follow their father
on his voyeur's journey through the text
toward many worlds *he* will likely never know.

who fell on their knees in hopeless cathedrals praying
for each other's salvation and light and breasts,
until the soul illuminated its hair for a second . . .

Yet here they are, showing there is no limit
to what might align *in the total animal soup of time*:
lace and nervousness and innocence,
in the faces of these four I've known
since all they could do was lie in a single place,
is captured here on paper and pressed against paper
where the faculties of the skull no longer admit
the worms of the senses;
and Ginsberg's vision (which is not his) is proven and disproven
in this instant of beauty which is and is no more;
and my daughters, sealed in this *Howl* as in a crevasse,
are at once released as on a huge, rising, balloon
whose sound at bursting will be so far away and small
we can only imagine how near and great it must be.

All italicized lines and phrases are from *Howl* by Allen Ginsberg.

No Beauty

This once, it must not turn beautiful.

No, I don't mean another bucket
dampened with crocodile tears,
musty and ripe for scattering
to the impoverished tens of thousands
rocking and keening in the dust,
to the millions starving
far from the smell of ink.

I mean no beauty close to home,
where every zero counts and burns each day:

My oldest daughter, fear in her eyes
when a man she's never met
reaches out along a crowded bar
to grab her wrist and hold,
to drill his stares at her face
while he wishes them hands at her crotch . . .

my adopted youngest, fresh from the triumph
that walking becomes for parent and child alike,
dreaming with no conception of dreams
the life she might have stayed with
in the arms of her child-mother,
wandering meek and filthy
the desert streets of Lima, Peru . . .

My wife, at work with her cooling dead,
occasionally two or three per shift:
how the time must come for the silenced or wailing
families to step outside the room,
to slough themselves away

that she may plug and wrap and bag
what had had a memory, a certain tone of voice.

Here is where we feel and know,
there is where we think and pretend.
Music and wit are not exempt from limit.
A terrible beauty is merely terrible.

Dirt

Dirt. There, and back there,
and over beyond. It holds,
lets grow, gullies, dries.
And here: my father's grave.

To My Daughters at My Death

Forgive me for grouping you again—
I have never done so lightly,
would speak to you singly now
if such would make more sense.
But I know you are gathered
in that clutch we made of you,
that clowder and murder and pride
we failed to see we were building
in the shine of all that we loved you, one by one.

Yet I am not here, and am not here
to say such glowing, tinted things.
You are reading me, I've guessed,
as a breathing quartet—four of anything
or a group engaged in music . . .
but there I go again, averting
even my dead eyes and trying
to divert your pooling thoughts
from this one sheet and all of me
you hold in hand. And hand. And hand. And hand.

The matter, I feel, is this:
what did I withhold as I tried to give,
what broke on the circles I presumed to close
with this second language I learned
when the first, my life, became a spell
too convoluted for my breaking?
Did I turn from you in the paltry name of art,
diminish you for the silly sham of wisdom?
My wise beauties—

      Heather of hardy flowering,
      Miranda of vision and wonder,
      Rebecca of searching and strength,
      Catherine of purity—

                 my wise beauties,
where have we left ourselves now that we're possessed
by the separate worlds we'd only feared or ignored,
now that I have no hand to touch your hands?

So much I missed of all you did and thought,
but now I miss it all: raise or lower your eyes
in trust or question or anger, and remember
I will not see. And wonder, can there be such sights
wherever I might be now? Do I still know
the shading and shifting of light in the delicate iris?
Pray for me, who never taught you how to pray,
that such a chilling, shivering thing might be.

Stone as Stone

Abjuring Political Poetry

Some men will shoot an infant in the face.
There, that's a start—near pentameter, even.
Has the world been bettered yet, or your mood?

The only mirror of horror is itself.
Art's a game when it thinks it shows the world
in actuality; art's a savior
when it stalks the world as art: stone as stone,
paint as paint, words as the music of words.

Here's a joke we children laughed at once:
What's the difference between a truckload
of bowling balls and one of dead babies?
You can't unload the balls with a pitchfork.

It's okay to laugh—that shows you sense the awfulness.
Imagine the hearer who did not get the joke:
No poem could reach him. No horror. No world.

Seattle Merry-Go-Round

Not what one would think, not the ready-made
comfort and stasis of endless whirling
seamlessly joined with dip and rise.
Not the cone-roofed, light-strung, calliopied building
heard and sighted from a distance. Not shrieking
children nor befuddled infants, not lovers with hands
goofily linked and rippling through
the down-up-down of adjacent horses—
lovers with groins triggered for the night
by the press of wooden backs, by the rhythmic
·thrusts against gravity and air . . .

Rather, the silence and almost-stillness of repair:
one woman's fingers probing with the delicate
sanders and brushes, touring the many hand-carved horses,
the one-of-a-kinds of goat, lion, dragon, and deer.
This triple circle of frozen beasts,
more playful than generals or gods in stone,
dwarfs its block-wide park at the city's eye.
Once bright and exotic with colors and shades
the woman can name like family, the carousel
rests worn and chipped by weekend leisure,
by idle hands and feet which gripped and picked and roamed.
The creatures' flanks have suffered heels,
their ears fingers, their saddles knees,
so that now Seattle's homeless gather daily—
however short these several summer weeks—
to watch the giant toy rekindled by lavender,
mauve, umber, brash chromatic yellow,
pine green, pearl, unspellable fuchsia and puce.

If a derelict lifts a hand toward the empty
one-ride midway, might she find her shaky, leathery claw
deserving of compare with the artist's
precisely wired fingers and wrist?
Or is analogy yet another province
traveled only by the fed and settled,
the owners of protein and vitamin B?

The painter talks with every watcher,
her focus deepened by distractions
born of contact. Here is art and politics
wed, beauty and hunger benignly balanced:
her paints and wages are public funds,
yet none of the homeless have wished her gone.

The wealthy come as well, down from their towers
to lounge in the sun that is everyone's dessert,
to shut off their brains for a while,
perhaps to rachet them far enough back to see
the simple, sacred coin in every child's palm—
boss-to-be with nose to the gleaming
windows of trinkets and sweets,
bum-to-be at his leaning, quavering shoulder.

Two Views of Charles Burchfield's *Six O' Clock*

For Adults: *Where the Painting Is*

You had thought the image was always somewhere else—
people distant or missing, buildings like castles
in air breathed out by exotic, extinct creatures.

But suddenly it is six o'clock, suddenly
Time steps toward you and says, so low, "You know me,
you have walked on my edge between evening and day,

gathered with family as the wall of dark grows hard."
And you see that all this was true, that the tired
moon sagging is a lone sister who shares your bed,

that the bowed heads at the table want food, want rest
you can offer them now that this is your place, your past
become present, this painting full of weight upon your chest.

Look to the blank foreground, whose odd angles speak best:
If your life lacks snow, those shadowed rollings are sea;
if your life is desert, dunes are these low-laid swells;
if your mountain days need mountains, here they are.

Look to the six stark roofs pretending sameness.
None is the same, except as each points its inverted v
skyward, lifting our eyes to that pale gauze
ff . . . what? Fog? Smoke? Light? *You* know. You *know*. Out loud.

For Children: *The Painting Comes Home*

So many paintings seem to be somewhere else
in space and time: people are lost in the background
or nowhere in sight, the buildings are like foreign castles.

But here we have a home and suppertime,
the air on that edge between day and evening,
the family gathered as the wall of dark grows hard.

These bowed head at the table simply want food, then rest.
Because you know this place, you can help them
find both. And because you are strong you can lead them

outside to show them so much more: the shadowed yard
whose rolling swells could be waves, dunes, or even mountains;
the six pointed roofs, each slightly different,
lifting toward smoke or fog or cloud;
and that moon, maybe sagging in its lonely wish
to come down and join you, maybe swelling tall
to light the yard and the house for us all.

Emily Dickinson Considers Basketball

In breathing—air is foremost still—
No perfect set of lungs
Makes headway in a vacuum—
Nor sings uncharted songs—

And yet each map is viable
According to its lands—
On fingertips the whorlings
Explain the hearts of hands—

And so this child—in alleyways—
Perfects his picks and shots—
While that one—God's own spotlight takes
To boast his body's cuts.

But both—give me the language—
To speak their passion's moves
As if the fact of motion
Made horses—talk with hooves—

Or angels sing with flutterings
Their tongues need not support—
The round and up and in and out—
Sufficient proof of art—

About the Author

Since 1981 Stephen Corey has published four full-length collections of poems and five chapbooks, as well as *Startled at the Big Sound: Essays Personal, Literary, and Cultural* (Mercer University Press, 2017). He has co-edited four books in three genres, including (with Warren Slesinger) *Spreading the Word: Editors on Poetry* (The Bench Press, 2001) and *Stories Wanting Only to Be Heard: Selected Fiction from Six Decades of* The Georgia Review (University of Georgia Press, 2012). His chapbooks, which included many of the poems that went into his full-length collections, are *Fighting Death* (1983) and *Attacking the Pietà* (1988), both from State Street Press; *Gentle Iron Lace* (1984), Press of the Night Owl; *Mortal Fathers and Daughters* (1999), Palanquin Press; and *Greatest Hits* (2000), Pudding House Press.

Corey's poems, essays, and reviews have appeared in dozens of periodicals, among them *American Poetry Review, Kenyon Review, Poetry, Shenandoah, Southern Review,* and *Yellow Silk*; and his work has been reprinted in numerous anthologies, including *Short Takes: Brief Encounters with Contemporary Nonfiction; The Poetry Anthology, 1912-2002;* and *Heart to Heart: New Poems Inspired by Twentieth-Century American Art.* He has been awarded writing fellowships from the arts councils of three states—Florida, South Carolina, and Georgia—as well as the Stanley W. Lindberg Award for Excellence in Literary Editing from the Rainier Writing Workshop MFA program at Pacific Luther University.

Corey was born in Buffalo, New York, in 1948, whence in 1952 his parents Dale and Julie moved him seventy-five miles south to Jamestown, about ten miles north of the Pennsylvania state line. After graduating from Jamestown High School in 1966—about thirty-five years after Lucille Ball—he lived in the Triple Cities area of New York while earning his BA and MA in English at Harpur College (now Binghamton University). In 1972 he returned to Jamestown and did newspaper work for *The Jamestown Post-Journal* for three years before moving to Gainesville, Florida, there completing a PhD in English at the University of Florida (1979) and co-founding *The Devil's Millhopper*, an independent poetry magazine. An English teaching position took him to the University of South Carolina until 1983, at which time he was hired as the assistant editor of *The Georgia Review* at the University of Georgia. He served the journal in various capacities for the next thirty-six years, holding the title of editor from 2006 until his retirement in 2019.